PENGUIN BOOKS

JACK HOBBS

JOHN ARLOTT, writer and broadcaster, was born in 1914 in Basingstoke, Hampshire. Cricket and wine correspondent of the *Guardian* and President of the Cricketers' Association since its foundation, he has been a policeman, B.B.C. producer, and a general instructor at the B.B.C. Training School. He has published a number of books of poetry, and has written and broadcast on cricket, wine, cheese, snuff, glass, aquatints, Hampshire, and the Isles of Scilly. He stood as Liberal candidate for Epping in the elections of 1955 and 1959. His unique career as both cricket correspondent of the *Guardian* and as B.B.C. cricket commentator, and a long friendship with Sir Jack Hobbs, enable him to give a full background to his portrait of one of the greatest of all opening batsmen.

JACK HOBBS

Profile of The Master

John Arlott

PENGUIN BOOKS

Penguin Books Ltd, Harmondsworth, Middlesex, England
Penguin Books, 625 Madison Avenue, New York, New York 10022, U.S.A.
Penguin Books Australia Ltd, Ringwood, Victoria, Australia
Penguin Books Canada Ltd, 2801 John Street, Markham, Ontario, Canada L3R 1B4
Penguin Books (N.Z.) Ltd, 182–190 Wairau Road, Auckland 10, New Zealand

First published by John Murray and Davis-Poynter 1981
Published in Penguin Books 1982

Made and printed in Great Britain by
Richard Clay (The Chaucer Press) Ltd,
Bungay, Suffolk

Valerie

(1932–1976)

in loving homage

Acknowledgements

THE PARTS of this book which do not come from the statistical and reporting chronicles of cricket are the product of observation of Sir Jack over almost forty years, and of conversations with him during twenty. Those talks were in themselves a memorable delight; they are the source of this book and of an affection which the writer, alas, lacks the skill to describe.

Thanks are due to P. G. H. Fender and Messrs. Chapman & Hall for permission to quote from *Defending the Ashes*; to David Frith and Nick Mason for help in tracing photographs; to Tom Blau of Camera Press; to Associated Press, Sport & General, and Central Press Photos for illustrations; and to members of the Cambridge Cricket Society for some valuable archival research.

Contents

To John Berry Hobbs
on his Seventieth Birthday

16 December 1952

There falls across this one December day
The light, remembered from those suns of June,
That you reflected, in the summer play
Of perfect strokes across the afternoon.

No yeoman ever walked his household land
More sure of step or more secure of lease
Than you, accustomed and unhurried, trod
Your small, yet mighty, manor of the crease.

The game the Wealden rustics handed down
Through growing skill became, in you, a part
Of sense, and ripened to a style that showed
Their country sport matured to balanced art.

There was a wisdom so informed your bat
To understanding of the bowler's trade
That each resource of strength or skill he used
Seemed but the context of the stroke you played.

The Master: records prove the title good:
Yet figures fail you, for they cannot say
How many men whose names you never knew
Are proud to tell their sons they saw you play.

They share the sunlight of your summer day
Of thirty years; and they, with you, recall
How, through those well-wrought centuries, your hand
Reshaped the history of bat and ball.

1

Jack & Sir John

JACK HOBBS—Sir John Berry Hobbs—was the poor man's son who became the finest batsman in the world, earned a knighthood, and bore it with innate modesty and dignity. His ability with a cricket bat was such that the title of 'The Master' settled upon him as the recognition of fact. He liked, though, to be known as 'Jack' and, if he had not been a famous sportsman, his personal qualities would still have made him outstanding within the circle of his acquaintance. He played a considerable part, too, in lifting the standing of his profession. To say that his knighthood was bestowed for batting does him less than justice. Nothing in his career is more significant than the fact that he was the first professional games player to be thus honoured. No one came nearer to defining the quality of his batting than Sir Pelham Warner when he said 'Jack Hobbs is a professional who bats exactly like an amateur'. Yet he was consciously and proudly a professional.

Although cricket made him important, it was less than the measure of his importance. His gift for batting may be described as genius, but genius can be devouring. Sometimes it leaves its possessor starved of all else; possessing a single transcendental capacity, but otherwise so limited—even mean—in character as to be virtually a two-dimensional figure. Jack Hobbs, though, was a warmly rounded and human person.

Since he constantly made news—indeed, cricket history—by his performances on the field, and because he was a modest man, the achievements of his playing days tended to obscure the quality of his personality. That became strikingly clear later, when his character could be observed divorced from his cricket. Yet it was never more important than during his playing days.

The first duties here are to state his standing and the reasons for it. He was, in all ways, a fine cricketer, but transcendent as a batsman. He scored more runs than anyone else in the first-class game, despite the facts that the next six men behind him played over longer periods; that he did not play at that level until he was twenty-two, then lost some six seasons to war, illness and injury, and refused several overseas tours. The weight of Jack Hobbs's run-scoring is of historic importance; but it misses the essence of his cricket. He had all the gifts of the great batsman. They included the qualities of understanding and sensitivity to a degree which made him unique. Others scored faster; hit the ball harder; more obviously murdered bowling. No one else, though, ever batted with more consummate skill than his, which was based essentially on an infallible sympathy with the bowled ball. Although he could improvise with quite impish virtuosity, it is no exaggeration to say that frequently—even generally— the spectator felt that the stroke he played seemed so natural as to be inevitable—or as if a choreographer had designed it as the rhythmically and poetically logical consequence of the bowler's delivery. It must be said, too, that while he was unwavering in his professional integrity, his batting was always honestly relevant to the game in which it belonged, and instinct with joy: he never made runs for the sake of runs, nor broke records for the sake of breaking records: and laughter was never far below the surface of his play.

His cricket had three distinct peaks of performance. In his early days his stroke-play had all the heady prodigality of richly endowed youth. In maturity he was the most completely rounded batting technician the game has ever known. In what was, by cricketing standards, old age—he scored a chanceless century against the County Champions at the age of fifty-one—his profound understanding of his craft compensated to an amazing degree for the deterioration of eye, mobility and muscle.

If, for the cricket enthusiast, the significance of Jack Hobbs lies in his scores, it must be remembered that enthusiasts in every field tend to be blinkered. As C. L. R. James wrote, and took as his theme, in *Beyond a Boundary* 'What do they know of cricket who only cricket know?' On the other hand, those who regard sport as unimportant and, for that reason, would consider Jack Hobbs unimportant, underestimate not merely the man, but sport also.

Hazlitt, who was a sound judge of the distinction between major and minor matters, wrote perceptively in his obituary of John Cavanagh, the fives player— 'When a person dies who does any one thing better than any one else in the world, which so many others are trying to do well, it leaves a gap in society.' That essay continued, relevantly to the present theme— needing merely the transposition of name and game to apply perfectly to Jack Hobbs—

He who takes to playing at fives has no other thought, from the moment the game begins, but that of striking the ball, of placing it, of *making* it. This Cavanagh was sure to do. His eye was certain, his hand fatal, his presence of mind complete. He could do what he pleased, and he always knew exactly what to do. He saw the whole game and played it. He had equal power and skill, quickness and judgement. He did his work with the greatest ease; never took more pains than was necessary; and while others were fagging themselves to death, was as cool and collected as if he had just entered the court. He had no affection, no trifling. He was a fine, sensible, manly player, who did what he could, but that was more than anyone else could even affect to do. There was not only nobody equal, but nobody second to him.

Because Jack Hobbs was himself; because his ambition was 'to be a cricketer'—and much lies in the complete simplicity of that aim—and because he had the inborn aptitude to do that, the story of his life is one of natural consequence: yet he made two quite spontaneous comments about his career. 'It really surprised me' and 'I have always been very grateful'.

He was the best kind of self-made man: independent, often making decisions alone; at need, self-sufficient; yet too affectionate by nature to be a solitary. No one taught him to play cricket; he never had an hour's coaching in his life, nor more than the occasional piece of advice. Yet he was, in every way, a complete batsman. No one ever gave him any guidance on his relations with the autocrats who ruled the cricket of his early days; nor how to deal with Indian princes; nor how to behave as a public hero; nor how to bear himself as Sir John Hobbs; nor how to conduct a competitive business with no previous business experience. In all these fields he succeeded with a quiet, almost—but not absolutely—urbane sensibility.

It has never been unusual for young men from humble backgrounds to become successful professional cricketers. It has been happening since at least the days of Hambledon; and it happens still. In the heyday of the county game, from about 1890 until 1914, they came in numbers and with high talent from the pits, the mills, the factories and the farmlands. All through that period, though, whatever playing success they might achieve, they remained a distinct, unbridgeable class below the amateurs who effectively controlled the game. Like their grooms, gamekeepers and footmen, the ruling class addressed cricket professionals by their surnames. Their futures were as umpires, coaches, groundsmen or publicans.

All that has changed: in part Jack Hobbs changed it: certainly he personified the change. In this he was the creature of historic incidence. When he first went to The Oval it was in the humble capacity of ground-staff boy in the almost feudal world of Edwardian cricket. He lived to be the first professional in modern times to lead an official England team on to the field against Australia; and, in 1953, his knighthood marked full circle of that social revolution. Others, like Sydney Barnes and Cecil Parkin, rebelled—not violently, but positively—against the autocracy. They were not so much defeated as pushed aside. The establishment stronghold was not to be taken by frontal catapult fire. Indeed, it was never to be taken at all; it exists now. The main current of social progress may have passed it by; but in that process it opened ways past it; and, with due respect for the citadel, Jack Hobbs moved round it to a position of fresh respect for himself and his kind. Once, in conversation, Walter Hammond, who, of course, changed from professional to amateur and as such captained England, asked Jack directly if he would have liked to become an amateur. There was no doubting the sincerity of his reaction—

> Oh, no; you see, I don't think I had it in me. I just wanted to be a professional cricketer; that made me quite happy and, if I had my time over again, I would want to do the same thing.

On a few occasions Jack Hobbs captained his county team; once, when Arthur Carr was absent ill, England. He did so with full understanding and competence. On other occasions he said little unless asked; but once at least, when requested, he directed a Test match against Australia and it was won.

He was financially successful; more, he was completely materially contented. A religious and a moral man, he had too much humour and humanity ever to be smug: he was a devoted husband and conscientious father and, because he was deeply compassionate, he suffered sadnesses. He sometimes carried modesty to the length of humility; he felt that he was lacking in profundity; but he was unquestionably a good man.

2

Cambridge Boy

THE LIFE of Jack Hobbs fell into five distinct phases, only the first two of major narrative importance or of uncertainty, before the processional successes. Those cover the years until he reached the Surrey ground staff, and his achievement in establishing himself on the highest level so rapidly, which held greater significance than it would have done in any other period. Both reflected his own frequent comment—'It doesn't matter how good a good batsman is, he still needs luck.' For the rest, there was the peak—justly called genius— of his first ten, pre-war, seasons with Surrey; the even more amazing high plateau of his post-war mastery; and the final old age, part anxious, part relaxed.

It is difficult now to appreciate that, but for a few fortunate chances, Jack Hobbs might never have played county cricket; or at least might only have done so so much later that the story would have been significantly altered. Nowadays a player of such capacity would be discovered—like Denis Compton or Colin Milburn—by some county's representative before he was out of school. In the next step he would be registered, and might be in a county team at seventeen. It is both facile and inaccurate to regard Jack Hobbs's progress to the Surrey staff as the 'log cabin to White House' kind of Victorian success story. He was twenty-two before he played in a county cricket match, which was such a waste of years of talent, and formative experience as to amount to injustice: his own reaction was one of gratitude that he reached it at all: but, once there, he still had anxieties.

Although his father was not an outstanding performer, Jack Hobbs, like most great games players, was brought up in a household imbued with the atmosphere of the game. Born in Cambridge on 16th December, 1882, he was the first of twelve children of John Cooper Hobbs and his wife, formerly Flora Matilda Berry. According to the birth certificate his father was then a slater's labourer, and the family was living with his mother's parents at 8 Brewhouse Lane, the workman's cottage of Elijah Berry, described at different times as baker, shoemaker and labourer. It was indeed what Jack Hobbs called 'a humble beginning'. Brewhouse Lane, which was demolished during the nineteen-thirties, lay in the angle between East Road and Norfolk Street. The boy was christened John Berry Hobbs, the first christian name for his father, the second for his mother's family.

Soon afterwards, his father achieved his unspectacular but most genuine ambition to become a professional cricketer, as a net bowler and occasional umpire on the staff at Fenner's, the University ground. In short, he became one of the army of college and University servants who in those days were content to spend their lives in that poorly paid security. Soon the local directories show 'J. Hobbs, cricketer' living first in Norfolk Terrace and then in Rivar Place, both near Brewhouse Lane, on the east side of Cambridge; and within a brisk run of Parker's Piece, the public playing ground which was to feature so importantly in Jack Hobbs's career, and where The Hobbs Pavilion now stands.

Jack Hobbs was by nature a gentle, uncomplaining

person but he was deeply conscious of his 'lowly upbringing'. He was too fond of his parents to reproach them for their circumstances. Nevertheless, he resented what he felt to be the inferiority of a back street cottage; and he never forgot those days. All his life they remained the yardstick of his gratitude for the prosperity and advantages he subsequently earned and enjoyed. Much of his effort to succeed sprang from the determination to provide for his children the background of security and opportunity he never knew in his own childhood.

The decision to make cricket the vehicle for that success was an inheritance. He had not only a deep affection, but a profound respect, for his father. The two were similar: both had the same compact, essentially neat, physique; and both were quiet in manner. Like Jack himself in later years, too, the elder Hobbs cared so deeply for cricket that he found it difficult to discuss a career in the game with his sons. No one else in any generation of the family made any mark on the game. John senior 'knew his place' in the world of the University. He understood that he could not take his boy to work with him, nor teach him the game in the helpful circumstances that existed there. Obliquely, though, in conversation at home he instilled a love of it, painting the life of the county professional in the glowing colours of unmalicious envy.

Significantly, Jack Hobbs insisted that he took to cricket 'naturally': he once put it—'I didn't think of playing for England or anything like that, but it seemed to me the best way I could make a decent living.' There was, too, the impressive local example of a successful cricketer in Tom Hayward; regarded with veneration by all cricketers, but especially by the lesser lights of his profession, like Hobbs senior. Hayward was the towering hero of Jack Hobbs's generation of

Cambridge boys who used to run to the public library in the evenings of Surrey matches to read his score.

It is not simple, in the latter half of the twentieth century, to appreciate the stature of Tom Hayward in the Cambridge of the eighteen-nineties. He was a typical figure of the Victorian age, when provincial towns produced and cherished their own great men. His ancestry was impeccable. His father and grandfather—both named Daniel—were cricketers of distinction in Cambridge who went on to play for Surrey, and his father had returned to take charge of Parker's Piece, the historic centre of 'Town'—and some 'Gown' —sport in Cambridge. His uncle and namesake, the first Tom Hayward, was generally considered the finest of all Cambridge cricketers until the rise of 'Young Tom'. The younger man justified his breeding. He was established now as run-scorer for Surrey and England: and, without much doubt, the best professional batsman in the country. Cricket history records him as one of the finest of all players of fast bowling. He was a national figure but, simultaneously and in quite different character, a local personality. He came home to Cambridge to live the non-working winter which was the proud mark of the successful nineteenth-century professional; and, when he walked the streets of his native town, strong and steady-looking with his curly-brimmed bowler, heavy moustache and a watch-chain stretched across his waistcoat, he was conscious that heads turned to look at him with respect. He was also, typically of his kind, conscious of his obligations to his public; and at the end of each cricket season he brought a team of county cricketers to play the pick of Cambridge town players for some local charity.

Tom Hayward was to have a considerable influence on Jack Hobbs's career; but not, except when they batted together, on his method of playing. The younger man's technique was not merely splendidly rich, but eminently correct. Once, when he was a small boy, his father bowled to him for a few minutes. Youngsters in his circumstances had no pads, of course; and he recalled that his father 'bowled either an off break or the one that floated away'—and 'I could sense the spin'. In an early intimation of his understanding of bowling, he took evasive action to protect his shins, whereupon, in the only item of instruction he ever received, his father called 'Don't draw away'. Certainly in after years he moved assuredly into off-spin and inswing.

Occasionally his mother made up a meal which he took to his father on the Jesus College ground, when briefly he had the opportunity to watch the undergraduates batting. He once remarked 'Yes, I suppose I copied the undergraduates—though some of them used to put in a flourish or two that I cut out.' When he was ten, his father, who was acting as a stand attendant for the match between the University and the touring Australian side at Fenner's, took him in to see it. Ranjitsinhji and Stanley Jackson were both in the University team and made considerable impressions on the enthusiastic boy.

Chiefly, though, he learnt in the only true fashion: by playing. Although the headmaster was sympathetic, there was little organised cricket at his church elementary school where football 'goals' were painted on the playground walls. His first match was as a late replacement for an absentee in the Jesus College choir team. At twelve he was captaining the St. Matthew's Church boys' team in evening matches and batting well enough to score twenties regularly. He played at night until the light went, but he was early about in the morning, working in a private house, cleaning shoes and silver, clearing and laying fires, carrying coal or doing odd jobs, for half-a-crown a week towards the strained family budget: there were seven younger children at home. During the holidays he helped his father, who was now the groundsman on the Jesus College ground; and, at thirteen, he left school to work as a college servant for seven-and-sixpence a week. There was compensation in slow progress towards the career which he felt called him; and, in his enthusiasm, he used to get up at six in the morning and walk to Parker's Piece for a practice session. He was beginning to stand out among his contemporaries. Already, indeed, he had his first follower, a youngster who worked on the local weekly paper. If the idea of his first century attracted Jack, it seemed even more important to his supporter. In due course he seemed on the way to it when, at 90, he was given out to what, sixty years afterwards, he still regarded as a grotesque lbw decision. His follower was even more indignant. He could not give the batsman the century he deserved, but the next issue of the local paper contained the score entry 'J. Hobbs not out 90'.

He himself believed afterwards that it was in 1901 that he was first convinced that he would achieve his ambition. It saw his first century—for Ainsworth against Cambridge Liberals—and an invitation to play, as an amateur, for Cambridgeshire against Hertford-shire. He felt nervous of the professionals, fearful they would think it presumptuous that the son of one of their own kind should play as an amateur. Neverthe-less, going in at number nine, he made 30 and shared in the highest partnership of the innings.

For years he had faithfully watched the match between Tom Hayward's team and the local side. This time one of the Cambridge team failed to turn up, young Hobbs was standing by and he jumped at the chance to make up the number. He scored 26 not out; but his father, standing umpire, took most pleasure from the convincing way he played the bowling of Hayward himself, who was good enough to take a hundred wickets in a first-class season. To the young man, however, his most significant advance—although he spoke about it to no one, it remained always in his mind—was that this was the point at which he began to know how he made his runs. If one adjective were to be chosen to define the batting of Jack Hobbs it probably should be 'understanding': when he was eighteen he realised that he understood.

The humdrum job at Jesus College was leading nowhere, though it left him with an enduring partisan loyalty to the college. In the summer after his nineteenth birthday he applied for, and got, the job of assistant professional at Bedford Grammar School. It entailed heavy work on the ground and constant bowling in the second eleven nets and, not at this point so wirily strong as he was to become, he found it dispiriting and exhausting. As some compensation, when he went with the team to umpire in their match with St. Paul's, he had his first sight of London.

At the end of the term he went home to Cambridge and earned his first match fee—ten shillings—when he scored 119 for Royston against Hertfordshire Club and Ground. He was delighted by his father's pleasure at this performance; and it was made the more indelible by the fact that John Cooper Hobbs, who guided his son, Jack Hobbs, towards cricket, died a week afterwards. Tom Hayward brought down a team to play a match for the widow's benefit; but Jack, in conventional Victorian mourning for his father, did not even consider playing. Neither could he bring himself to approach Tom Hayward. It is the measure of his shyness, and of the awe in which he held the great man that, even after they had been going in first for Surrey for two seasons, he could not bring himself to invite his senior partner to his wedding. Now, however, Francis Hutt, a friend of his father and another Jesus College servant, who used to score for the cricket team, spoke to Tom Hayward on his behalf and asked if he would look at Jack with a view to recommending him for a trial at The Oval.

That was agreed and, in due course, Jack Hobbs presented himself at Parker's Piece. There Hayward, and Bill Reeves, of Essex, bowled at him while for twenty minutes he paraded every stroke he had—and contrived not to get out. Tom Hayward mumbled casually that he would see about a trial at The Oval in the following Spring: but there was nothing more definite than that.

Meanwhile, Jack took over his father's duties until another groundsman was appointed, when he found another job with the College—and waited. The devoted Mr Hutt, concerned enough to feel that a second string approach should be made to another county, accordingly wrote to Essex, who had something of a tradition of recruiting Cambridgeshire cricketers, to ask if they would consider another. If they had, the history of English cricket might have been different. In the event, Essex never answered the letter. Indeed, one must wonder how many county secretaries in 1903 would have paid serious attention to a recommendation from a college servant. All now depended on Tom Hayward. The Hobbs household was desperately poor and Jack, the eldest son, was conscious of his responsibility to his mother and the other children. Indeed, if the letter from The Oval had not come—that is, if Jack Hobbs had not been a boy from the Cambridge of Tom Hayward—it must be possible that sheer deadweight of poverty would have smothered his cricket.

In due course the summons from Surrey arrived and, on 23 April 1903, the twenty-year-old Hobbs was one of a dozen young men who presented themselves to the county coach. He was the only one asked to remain for the subsequent trial matches and, on the second day, he was bidden to the secretary's office and offered a contract to qualify for Surrey at a salary of thirty shillings a week during the season and a pound a week during the winter. He returned to Cambridge in such a whirl of relief and elation that he even dared to tell Tom Hayward his news. He did not know until long afterwards that the older man persuaded the Surrey club to pay him a £10 bonus at the end of the season to ease his family's situation. That enabled him to send more home to his mother; indeed, he did his best to maintain her for the rest of her life.

By modern standards it seems ludicrous that he could not go home during the winter; but the rules governing residential qualification were so strictly enforced at that time that official visits were paid every few weeks to ensure that the players recruited from outside their registered counties were duly camped and cramped in their declared lodgings.

So Jack Hobbs spent two dutiful qualifying summers when he might better have been playing first-class cricket. In his first match as a member of the staff—for Surrey Colts against Battersea—he scored a duck. After that few who saw him bat had any doubt of his quality. He tended to be shy; as respectful of authority as Cambridge had taught him to be; hesitant about addressing the established professionals; but when he picked up a bat, he was secure. In his first qualifying summer he was top of the batting averages for Surrey Colts. During the second, when he averaged 43.9 for the Club and Ground, he was put out to grass with Cambridgeshire. There he found exciting touch. After 54 and 52 against Oxfordshire, he heard that Surrey were having him watched in the next match, with

Norfolk. He made 92 in two-and-a-half hours—which he felt was too slow, but probably convincing. Basil Cozens-Hardy, one of the Norfolk bowlers who came in for some punishment in the course of that innings, went to his grave believing that the number of legside fours he suffered won Jack Hobbs's Surrey place. There was, though, already much—and even more convincing —evidence of his talent. With two centuries against Hertfordshire, he led the Cambridge batting averages with a figure of 58; and there were references in the national press to his brilliant promise. Cricket had happened to Jack Hobbs: Jack Hobbs was about to happen to cricket.

3

The Surrey Player

AT THE START of the 1905 season Jack Hobbs became
a qualified Surrey player. At that time there were
twenty-two professionals on the Oval staff; while, of
eighteen amateurs, five had virtually irrefutable—and
three more, reasonable—claims to selection when available. Twelve of them played Test cricket for England;
and Surrey finished fourth in the Championship that
season. So, although the 'new' player had batted
impressively against Norfolk when he was watched, he
was by no means an automatic first team choice.

Once again events fell into a happy pattern for him.
The county's first match was a pipe-opener against the
Gentlemen of England beginning on Easter Monday.
By historic coincidence, the Gentlemen's side was
captained by W. G. Grace, now nearing the end of his
mighty career; and Surrey by Tom Hayward. They
were the first two batsmen, as Jack Hobbs was the third,
to reach a hundred centuries in first-class cricket. It was
fitting, too, that the first appearance of the man who
was to inherit the position of the finest English
batsman, should be in a match with his two pre-
decessors, for, between Grace's decline at the end of
the century and his own, Tom Hayward stood at the
top of the English game. Similarly, Jack Hobbs was to
play with and against Walter Hammond and Donald
Bradman in another historic overlapping.

His name was posted among the fourteen 'from whom'; and remained there when two amateur batsmen, for reasons possibly not unconnected with the atrociously cold weather, intimated that they were not available. None of the four men who had generally opened the innings with Tom Hayward in the previous season was playing. The ageing Bobby Abel was on the verge of retirement and did not relish so bleak a day; neither Albert Baker nor Fred Holland was fit; and John Raphael, who had been the most successful of them, was not available until after the University match. Still Ernie Hayes, an established batsman who had gone in first, was in the side. By the final stroke of fortune, in the absence of the new captain, Lord Dalmeny, the decision fell to Tom Hayward. He, probably out of consideration, certainly more wisely than he knew, and much to the young man's grateful relief, took Jack Hobbs in first with him. He cannot have dreamt that he was initiating a great opening partnership.

Each got away with a quick single in the first over, but the pitch was awkward and the Gentlemen's opening bowlers, George Beldam and Walter Brearley, were admirably equipped to exploit it. They put out Surrey for 86. Jack Hobbs was caught at slip off Beldam for only 18; but that was enough to make him joint top scorer of the innings with Ernie Hayes. When the Gentlemen batted Neville Knox, in his turn, made the ball lift awkwardly and Surrey went in again only 29 behind.

Overnight—44 in an hour—and next morning, Jack Hobbs batted with a commanding ease which was a revelation to those who had not seen him play before. He seemed to be taking a century as he willed when he pulled a ball from Walter Brearley that was too near his legs for that stroke and skied it to Frank Crawford at square leg. As he passed Brearley on his way out, that hearty extrovert growled 'I should drop that stroke if I were you.' He did not drop it; in fact, as he grew older, he scored an increasing proportion of his runs with it; but as he said 'I learnt to play it properly—to a short ball outside the off stump.' His 88 was the highest score of the game—on either side—and *Wisden's* report ended with 'the feature of the match was the batting of Hobbs whose first appearance in first-class cricket was an emphatic success. He scored his 88 in two hours and only made one real mistake.'

A week afterwards Essex, the county that refused Hobbs a trial, came to The Oval. He made 28 in a small Surrey first innings but, in the second—with a borrowed bat—155 at almost a run a minute. This was the authentic Hobbs; and both spectators and players were moved by the dashing certainty of his batting. At the end of the match he caught his fellow Cambridge man, Bill Reeves, in the deep; the crowd raced across the ground, cheering and calling his name and, in the spontaneous fashion of earlier times, as the players came off the field, his captain, Lord Dalmeny, gave him his county cap.

The following match was against Hampshire and, after scoring only 6 in the first innings, he made a valuable 43—more than the margin of Surrey's narrow win—in the second.

Next day the Australians came to The Oval. This was undeniably a strong side, beaten in the Test rubber only by, arguably, the most powerful of all English teams. Captained by Joe Darling, they had Victor Trumper, Monty Noble, Clem Hill, Warwick Armstrong, Reggie Duff, Jim Kelly and Frank Laver. Jack Hobbs rated their opening bowler, 'Tibby' Cotter, on that tour, the fastest bowler he ever faced. He had some uneasy moments against him, but he made 94 before Clem Hill, with only a single stump to aim at from the third man boundary, hit it and ran him out. It was not a flawless innings, but it was an aggressive one; no other Surrey batsman scored more than 24 of their 225; but that run-out grieved him all his days: so deeply that he never quite knew whether he resented it out of disappointment, or because he thought it an inaccurate decision. He was caught off Cotter for only 1 in the second innings: and, no doubt, learnt much from watching Hayward make a century.

No newcomer could be expected to continue in such fashion. The tangle of new experiences, impressions, excitement, were bound to have a disturbing effect on concentration. He did little in the following four matches apart from a serviceable 40 against Warwickshire; indeed, returning to Cambridge for the first time as a Surrey cricketer, he was caught at the wicket for nought. Then, at the beginning of June, in the return with Essex, he made a confident and fluent 102. So far from re-establishing his confidence, that innings was followed by a run of poor scores. Briefly at the end of July he seemed to recover his zest and touch with a competent 58 in the second match with the Australians. Immediately afterwards he made a bright 75 not out, when he and Hayward gave Surrey a ten wicket win over Middlesex with a fast-scoring, unbroken opening stand of 168 in what had been, until then, a bowlers' match. Apart from those two occasions, however, he did not play an innings of as many as 40 in the two months between the second century against Essex and the end of the season.

The truth was that he had no reserves of strength or stamina and, as he had done at Bedford School, he became easily and deeply fatigued. Thirty years afterwards the young Len Hutton found the strain of the six-day cricketing week unsupportable; and he, too, had to be 'rested'. He, though, never lost form as Jack Hobbs did in 1905 when he scored only 150 runs—72 of them in three innings—in eight matches.

This was the worst time he ever had in cricket, and always afterwards the memory of it coloured the advice he gave to young men who wanted to take up cricket as a career. He had 'bad trots' subsequently but never one so protracted nor which caught him so unprepared: and later, of course, he was established beyond question. Until now his cricket had been a steady progression, a series of mounting achievements. Now came this quite bewildering setback for which he knew no remedy. Technically, weariness had affected the coordination of eye, mind and muscles sufficiently to make that minute but crucial difference between the timed and middled stroke and one which was mistimed or edged. The margin of error between middle and edge of a cricket bat is, after all, only two inches. That is a truth which never enters a batsman's mind when he is in form; when he is off, it can become an obsessive hazard. In a real 'trot' the problem rapidly becomes more psychological than technical. This is something the casual part-time player or the follower of cricket often does not understand. For several reasons only the professional cricketer —or career amateur—can experience this feeling; first because his livelihood—which seems like life—is at stake; secondly, it goes on, unrelieved, day after day.

Indeed, the stress is magnified for the man in the first-class game when he has to wait two or three days—perhaps more, over a match-free period—before he has the chance to try again. Nets may help, but they are no substitute for confidence—nor for the luck the out-of-form player needs. At a time like this the cricketer recognises his loneliness. Cricket is loosely described as a team game; yet in essence it is the most individual combat of all. There is no other isolation in sport so complete as that of the batsman as he faces a bowler supported by ten fieldsmen. The starkest form of that loneliness is suffered by the opening batsman.

Once distress infects a player it intensifies; anxiety and weariness feed on one another; worry-tensed muscles exaggerate difficulties, investing normal stroke-reaction with peril: all at once, what had seemed as natural as breathing becomes impossible. Luck, too, invariably is involved. Bad fieldsmen catch the un-catchable; the victim gets the one ball of the day that lifts, squats or moves; a good umpire nods; a movement behind the bowler at the moment of delivery breaks concentration. One modern player put it—'On this tour I have been out in every possible way except "top hat fell on wicket".'

The 'bad trot' is a batsmen's disease. The case that is talked of is invariably one that is cured. If it is not, the player simply goes out of the game. Then no one speaks of a 'bad trot'. It is said 'he was not good enough', 'he could not stand the strain of the first-class game', 'he simply was not sound' or, even 'he did not try'. All those may be half-truths. Too often a combination of ill luck and psychological pressure exaggerates relatively unimportant flaws of method. Certainly instances can be recalled of players who seemed to have all the qualities for success but whose self-belief was so undermined by a bad trot that their technique visibly deteriorated. In 1975 one of the most promising young English batsmen of the last two decades left the game as a result of the cruellest form of 'bad trot'—the long one. After a couple of good seasons it set in, eroding his confidence and, therefore, his performance. Yet every time he seemed to have failed irretrievably, he played an innings which showed his potential so brightly as to renew hope. In the end he accepted that bruising denial of his true quality; he called it a day.

While, ultimately, only the player himself can pull out of one of these spells, it can affect an entire team, especially when a key batsman is afflicted. Some of the happiest and most convivial occasions of any county cricket season celebrate the occasion when a batsman pulls out of a 'long trot'.

Jack Hobbs found the process cruelly cumulative. 'Sometimes after I was out I would go and sit down in the dressing-room without taking my pads off, and think, and I thought I should never make another run.' His arm ached from throwing—the boundaries at The Oval are the longest in the country—he lost his eagerness in the field and, when he fumbled out of weariness, there was always some spectator quick to jeer. Until the end of his playing days he was deeply sensitive to unfriendly crowd reactions. Eventually his batting was so affected that he was twice out—most uncharacteristically—'hit wicket', which only happened to him three times in the next twenty years. The Surrey club were confident of his ability, but they became worried, not only by his loss of form, but by the effect it had on him. In the attempt at rehabilitation he was moved down the order, reinstated as an opener, dropped, and then recalled for the last match of the season. It was to be played at The Oval with its good batting wicket, against Leicestershire, one of the weaker bowling sides; and there was nothing 'in' it for either county. Jack Hobbs was to bat in the 'easy' position of number five. It was all therapeutically intended; but, with the savage irony of the 'bad trot', he was bowled by an indifferent change bowler named Whitehead for 9—out of a Surrey total of 549 for six. His ill fortune was underlined, and his winter preoccupations were increased, by the fact that Fred Holland went in first and shared an opening partnership of 112 with Tom Hayward.

Wisden, reviewing the Surrey season, observed encouragingly:

> At the opening of the season it was known that a good deal was hoped of him. His early play exceeded all expectations and by the end of May he had firmly established his reputation, his scoring for three or four weeks being extraordinary; it cannot be said that he kept up his form.

No one appreciated the validity of the final phrase better than he. In comparative terms his 1317 (at 25.82) in all matches put him seventh in the Surrey batting averages: in Championship matches, though, his 1004 at 24.48 placed him ninth. In six matches, including his first four, he had scored 638 runs, in the remaining twenty-four, 679. He would not have been the pragmatist he was if he had not recognised that the question for him—and Surrey—was whether the true Hobbs was the batsman of the six matches, or the twenty-four.

There was no parent or older man to counsel or reassure him that winter in the lodgings in Fentiman Road that he shared with another ground staff lad, the cheerful Joe Bunyan. Jack Hobbs was thoughtful and anxious: clear-sighted enough to recognise cricket for a perilous career. He did his utmost to keep fit, walking long distances across London, playing badminton and football; once experimenting with a 'body building' system. Even then, the philosophical strain which was so important a part of his character in later years was strong in him. Above all, and for all his modesty and quietness, his resolve was firm, as was to be reflected over the years in his outstanding performances on difficult wickets and in apparently losing situations. He was undemonstratively, but highly combatively, resilient against odds. So he proved now.

4

Emergent Genius

JACK HOBBS established himself as a complete cricketer in talent, temperament and character in 1906. When that season began he had to demonstrate to himself, to the Surrey committee and to the general cricket world that his falling off in 1905 was not fundamental. He never forgot the encouragement of his fellow professionals, who understood better than any how he felt; but he had to prove himself by himself. Characteristically, he put his head down and played himself out of his troubles. Tom Hayward was an immense help and reassurance. The pair were never great talkers; Jack because he was shy of the older man; Tom Hayward because he was simply one who got on with his job. One explanation of their strength as a pair lay in their dissimilar styles. Tom Hayward personified the nineteenth century in his upstanding style. Tall and strong with a long rosy face, a slight stoop and sloping shoulders, he was essentially unhurried, dealing phlegmatically with the fastest bowling, his attacking strength in front-of-the-wicket strokes, driving with controlled power even on lively pitches. Jack Hobbs was to typify the 'modern' school, quick footed, forward or back, dealing with late swing, leg theory or the googly by fresh methods, involving, in particular, sophisticated on-side techniques.

They were to become, those two Cambridge men,

the finest opening pair cricket had yet known. For the moment, however, the younger had to re-establish his footing. He left nothing to chance, talked little; treated pre-season nets and the trial matches with absolute seriousness; but he was almost desperately eager to get to grip with his problem. Surrey's first match of the season was, once more, against the Gentlemen of England, with W. G. Grace and Tom Hayward the respective captains. Surrey batted second: Hayward and Hobbs opened their innings sedately enough, with 50 in a little over the hour before Hobbs was bowled by May for an unremarkable, but tidy, 29. Of their second innings *Wisden* reported—'Nothing in the game was quite so good as the batting of Hayward and Hobbs who, when Surrey went in with 235 to make, obtained 135 of this number in an hour and a half.' Hayward's share of the stand was 82, extras 11; Jack Hobbs, determinedly careful, relieved himself of most of his anxieties with a substantially slower, but eminently sound 85 not out in the eventual 237 for two. He and Hayward again made a steady 50 for the first wicket against Hampshire when Hobbs, with 79 and 69, for the first time made two scores of over fifty in a match. Then, within a fortnight of May, he removed all his doubts and those of any who watched. He made carefully certain of his ground. On the Leicestershire match, *Wisden* reported 'Hayward batting in brilliant and faultless style, the first wicket yielded 208 runs. Hobbs played thoroughly sound cricket'. Then, by way of 80 off Essex, to Worcester and a report which ran:

The outstanding feature of the game was the brilliant display of batting given by Hobbs on the first day. Second out at 194 he scored his 125 in less than two hours; Hayward though not so rapid in his methods, played correct, stylish cricket and with Hobbs put on 176 for the first wicket in an hour and forty-five minutes.

This time there was no tailing off; in the return with Worcestershire at The Oval, Surrey, needing 286 to win, lost their first four wickets for 112 before Hobbs (162) and J. H. Gordon scored the remaining 174.

When George Hirst and Schofield Haigh cut down Surrey for 113 on a difficult pitch at Sheffield, Jack Hobbs went in first and carried his bat for 38 without an observable mistake. At the end of the season, against Middlesex, Tom Hayward, with a painstaking 110 in the first innings, equalled C. B. Fry's figure of thirteen centuries in a season and beat Bobby Abel's record aggregate of 3309. On the last afternoon, in the effort to force a win, Jack Hobbs scored 103 at better than a run a minute; but those who followed him could not sustain the pace.

He thought that, at that time, he had most difficulty with well flighted slow left-arm bowling; and he lost his wicket to it often enough to suggest that his judgement was correct. If it was a weakness, he was soon to eradicate it; meanwhile he had addressed himself seriously to the matter in the nets. He was never a great believer in averages, but committees—and selectors—are; so he could contemplate with some comfort figures of 1913 at 40.70 in all Surrey matches (Hayward 3246 at 72.13); 1751 at 41.69 in the Championship, in which Surrey finished third, their best position for seven years.

Wisden, noting that 'In batting Hayward stood out by himself as the great player of the year', commented also that:

Hobbs and Hayes played splendidly and would have been far more talked about if they had been in any other eleven.

As it was Hayward overshadowed them. Hobbs more than bore out the expectations formed of him in 1905 and was one of the finest professional bats of the year. Good as he is, it is not in the least degree likely that he has yet reached his highest point.

He spent the winter of 1906–07 in full confidence and a newly entered state of matrimony.

Though county cricket may have been the limit of Jack Hobbs's early ambition, his sights were set higher by the end of 1906. He could hardly have nursed that hope in a less encouraging situation. Not for nothing was this called the Golden Age of cricket; and it was golden chiefly for batsmen, as many amateur as professional.

In 1907 South Africa came to England and lost a three-Test series by the single match finished. The English selectors used only twelve players in the rubber, including four of the rare, true all-rounders worth their places as batsmen or bowlers—in Len Braund, Jack Crawford, George Hirst and Gilbert Jessop—even without Stanley Jackson, who could have had the captaincy for the acceptance if he had been available. They left out, too, from the remarkable crop of all-rounders in the period, Wilfred Rhodes, B. J. T. Bosanquet and John Gunn who had been in the side which won the home rubber of 1905 against Australia, as well as Albert Relf and Ernie Hayes who had been to South Africa in 1905–06.

They chose as batsmen R. E. Foster—the captain—Tom Hayward, C. B. Fry and Johnny Tyldesley, while 'Dick' Lilley, the wicket-keeper, was third in the batting averages. Jack Hobbs can hardly have been considered. Among other batsmen not chosen were K. L. Hutchings, A. C. MacLaren, Percy Perrin, R. H. Spooner, Albert Knight, George Gunn, Joe Hardstaff,

David Denton, John Tunnicliffe, Lionel Palairet, Pelham Warner, A. O. Jones and F. L. Fane; while Ranjitsinhji was out of the country and not available for selection. So far as Jack Hobbs was concerned, three other Surrey men, Tom Hayward and Jack Crawford who were already in the England team; and Ernie Hayes, above him in the complete Surrey averages with 54 more runs and an average four better—two of whom were Test bowlers—would compete with him for a Test place.

That was the stronghold Jack Hobbs was setting out to conquer at the beginning of the 1907 season. It appeared all but impregnable. The best he could possibly hope was to win one of the—say—six batting places in the touring side for Australia in the winter of 1907–08. He was one of fourteen candidates. As a prerequisite he needed to be selected for Gentlemen *v* Players at Lord's, which would be virtually a Test trial. Despite his experience in 1905 it remained one of his pet superstitions that if he did not make a good start to the season he would never get going.

After such a fine finish to 1906, he made a bad start in 1907 with 2 in his only innings against Grace's XI; 8— but then 51 not out—against Northamptonshire; 6 against Essex. Then he seemed to settle into the season until he made 0 and 1 in the Whit Monday match with Nottinghamshire—the nearest he ever came to a 'pair' in his career. Recovering, he carried his bat for 60 out of 155 against Warwickshire on a bad Edgbaston wicket. In mid-June he and Tom Hayward put on a hundred for the first wicket in each innings of two consecutive matches—in fact within five playing days. In the next game he made 150 not out against Warwickshire, and was invited to play in both Gentlemen *v* Players matches, at Lord's and The Oval. *Wisden* observed simply 'Hobbs, on his form fully deserved the compliment of being picked for the professionals but he failed.' He failed, indeed; in both innings of both matches. At Lord's in the first innings Brearley—who had a good memory—bowled him for 2 with a straight ball that he tried to pull, but which kept low; and, in the second, had him caught at the wicket off a lifter for 9. At The Oval he made 5 and 19. It was some consolation that no one else except Hayward and Hirst made a large score at Lord's: but Whitehead (of Leicester), John Gunn, Archie MacLaren and R. A. Young all did well at The Oval: and only he failed completely four times.

Nevertheless, he was chosen to go to Australia; and that tour established him as a Test player for more than twenty years. Yet his very selection was the most remarkable stroke of good fortune he ever experienced. Of the twelve players who had appeared against South Africa, only three—Len Braund, Jack Crawford and Colin Blythe—were in the party for Australia. Comment on the party is best summarised by Major Philip Trevor the team manager, who—as would not be remotely contemplated today—also reported the tour for *The Daily Telegraph*. (He was in fact the only English journalist to cover it). His survey refers to discussion as to whether the team 'had a right to rank as a first, a second or a third eleven'.

A week before it was chosen, no one could have guessed its eventual composition. None of the four main batsmen of the home series was included; R. E. Foster could not go because of business commitments; while Tom Hayward and Johnny Tyldesley—like George Hirst and 'Dick' Lilley, too—would not accept the payment offered by MCC. F. S. Jackson, Gilbert Jessop and Archie MacLaren were not available; and surprisingly Pelham Warner (third in the first-class averages) was passed over for the captaincy. That went to A. O. Jones of Nottinghamshire (thirty-third in the averages) whom most would have regarded as at best a fifth choice after Warner, Foster, Fry and Jackson. The eventual party, indeed, contained only five of the twenty-two players who had taken part in Gentlemen-Players at Lord's. Only Blythe of the specialist bowlers against South Africa was picked; Neville Knox—who had been troubled by an injury—and Ted Arnold were left out. A case could have been made, too, for taking Reggie Spooner, John Gunn and Jack Sharp. *Wisden* commented:

> R. E. Foster and other amateurs found themselves unable to be away from England for the length of time involved and all hope of sending out a representative side had to be abandoned when Hayward, Hirst, Tyldesley and Lilley declined the terms offered them.

That passage continued 'It has been freely stated, and so far as one knows without contradiction, that C. B. Fry was not asked to go.' Written so near the event, that may have been justified. Fry, however, only made one overseas tour—to South Africa in 1895 after he came down from Oxford. Subsequently he refused several invitations on the grounds that he could not leave his commitments in England; that meant chiefly the training ship *Mercury*. During the winter of 1907–08, when he did not go to Australia, he was negotiating to take over *Mercury*; there is, though, nothing at this range to indicate which was cause and which effect. The final choice was A. O. Jones, S. F. Barnes, C. Blythe, L. C. Braund, J. N. Crawford, A. Fielder, F. L. Fane, J. Hardstaff, E. G. Hayes, J. B. Hobbs, J. Humphries, K. L. Hutchings, W. Rhodes, R. A. Young. It was agreed, too, that George Gunn, who was going to Australia for his health, 'should, at the discretion of the captain, play for the team, in the event of an emergency caused by illness or accident.'

In a wet summer no such batting figures were attained as Hayward's in the previous season; but Jack Hobbs with 2135 runs was one of only three batsmen— Hayward and Johnny Tyldesley were the others—to score over 2000; and with a figure of 37.45, he was eighth in the national averages.

Even so, and despite the defections, he was not an automatic selection. There was some discussion about him; Archie MacLaren—oddly in the light of his later enthusiasm—was critical of his batting; in truth he had reason to be, for in eleven innings in matches which MacLaren was playing, he had only once scored more than 25; a 72 against Lancashire in 1907 at The Oval, which was not one of his best performances. It seems likely that 'Shrimp' Leveson Gower, a Surrey player and an admirer from the start, ensured his choice.

Jack Hobbs could feel that his good luck ended when he boarded the ship for Australia. He soon discovered that he was a bad sailor; he suffered acutely from seasickness all his life; and on this first voyage he spent almost all his time in his bunk, and arrived in Australia drawn, weak and generally out of sorts.

There was no question of his being well enough to play in either of the first two matches when A. O. Jones and F. L. Fane both made centuries going in first. He was not fully fit, nor in practice, for the game with Victoria when his scores were 3 and 26 (Jones at the other end made 82); he was left out of the New South Wales fixture and against Queensland made 21. During that match Jones fell ill and was unable to play for two months. The fixture before the first Test was with 'An Australian Eleven' when Hobbs was left out and the only English innings was opened by Fane and Dick Young who made 55 between them. Although Jones was ill, he supervised the selection of the team, pressed home his belief that Young (the 'second' wicket-keeper) and Fane should go in first; and, exercising the discretion Lord's had granted him, called in George Gunn. Jack Hobbs felt, with some reason, that he had been given less than fair opportunity. Certainly three innings from a possible six matches prior to the first Test is hardly the chance to find form or win a place. More than once such a start has ruled a batsman out of an entire series. The need to keep the Test choices in full practice can prevent the out-of-form man ever playing enough to find form; and it is invariably harder to displace an established member of a team than to hold a place.

His seasickness and lack of form may explain leaving out Hobbs; but it is difficult to justify including George Gunn who had not played in a match at all. He was, of course, a Nottinghamshire colleague of Arthur Jones, who appreciated his quite considerable batting gift which might be said to amount to genius. The free-speaking Major Trevor gave it as his opinion that, but for his illness, George Gunn might well have been an original choice for the team. Certainly that was eventually confirmed by figures, for he was top of the English batting in both aggregate and average for the Test series. The plain fact is that the tour selection committee, undoubtedly influenced by Jones who was a strong and forceful character, brought in Gunn in preference to Hobbs or Hayes neither of whom had made runs. Once again, Jones's judgement was based on the evidence available to him. Whatever Jack Hobbs might have done against other opposition, his record in matches against Jones was of 235 runs in sixteen innings with a highest score of 36. Jones had never seen him play a good innings but he had seen George Gunn play many.

The decision to bring in the inexperienced 'Dick' Young, for his batting, in preference to Joe Humphries, a far sounder wicket-keeper, probably cost England the first Test, which they lost by two wickets in a tensely close finish. The tourists had two matches between the first and second Tests; against 'A Victorian XI' and the raffish-sounding if, by cricketing standards, unimportant Eighteen of Bendigo. On the assumption that Humphries would be brought into the Test side and that, after scores of 13 and 3, Young would not be played for his batting alone, there was a vacancy for a batsman which would be filled by either Hobbs or Hayes, neither of whom had yet made an appreciable score. Both of them had a single innings in each of the two intervening matches. Hobbs made 77 and 58; Hayes 98 and 53. Jack Hobbs was chosen for the Melbourne Test, because—according to Jack Crawford— 'Wilfred Rhodes and Len Braund pointed out he was so obviously a better player.' He was never again left out of an English Test team when he was fit and available in the twenty-three years until he announced his retirement from Test cricket.

As many capable players had already discovered, and as others were yet to do, a failure in a single match could be conclusive in a period so prolific in talent as Edwardian English cricket. Jack Hobbs had reached the English team for the first time in his life; and he set out with the quiet but single-minded determination and high skill which were his stock-in-trade to ensure that it was not the last. He described it as 'the sort of innings you have to play when you are playing for your place.' Major Trevor thought:

Hobbs from start to finish played almost faultless cricket. He scored slowly, it is true, but his caution was amply justified. He was always really master of the situation, but he showed his good sense by not presuming on the fact.

He made 83 in a little more than three hours; 28 in the second innings; and, in yet another savagely close finish, England won by one wicket.

Described before it left as 'a third team' Jones's side won only that one Test of the series, and were beaten four-one in the rubber. Yet, in three of the matches lost, they stood at times in probable winning situations; and, if they sometimes erred sadly in the field, they had the worst of some atrocious weather.

In the third Test Jack Hobbs made 26 in the first innings, was injured at the start of the second and returned only towards the end, in pain, to make 23 not out in a defeat which was something of an anti-climax. The fourth Test—at Melbourne again—was decided by the weather. England put out Australia on a good pitch for 214 and then had to bat on a genuine Australian 'sticky dog'. England were bowled out in 110 minutes for 105, of which Jack Hobbs made 57 in seventy minutes; otherwise only George Gunn (13) reached double figures. This innings was remembered by those who saw it as a vivid display of virtuosity. The ball was lifting and angling unpredictably; and only Jack Hobbs could survive on it. Jack Crawford thought:

> You would never have dreamt this was a man playing in only his third Test match; he seemed so mature and so certain. It was a safe bet that anyone would get an edge within a couple of overs; but Jack stayed there for over an hour and he hardly made a mistake. Either he let the ball go past without making a stroke at it or he hit it in the middle. Few men—even he—can ever have played a better bad wicket innings.

Jack himself was piqued by his second innings 'duck', caught and bowled off a ball which 'stopped'. With 72 and 13 in the last Test he finished second to George Gunn in the English Test averages.

English cricket in 1908 had the almost purely domestic season which never occurs nowadays. The Gentlemen of Philadelphia toured the country but there were no Test matches and, to the declared satisfaction of many, the counties were able to concentrate on the Championship.

Surrey once again were third in the table; without Neville Knox their bowling was not quite strong enough to offer a consistent challenge to Yorkshire or Kent. Jack Hobbs now, though only twenty-six, an established county senior, scored five Championship centuries. He did not start the season well. In Surrey's opening Match, as usual against the Gentlemen of England—which was W. G.'s last first-class appearance that year—he was bowled by Walter Brearley for 0. He soon recovered with a murderous 161 off Hampshire.

In the final figures only three batsmen scored more runs than his 1904. Tom Hayward was the only man in the country to make over two thousand; Alan Marshal, the Australian, in his first full season with Surrey, hit spectacularly and made 1931; David Denton of Yorkshire, 1925. It was indicative of that county's batting power that three of the leading four were Surrey players.

In every season Jack Hobbs played one or two innings which were not merely numerically large but, in some facet of his varied genius, beyond the capacity of ordinary men. In 1908, he played one against Kent at Blackheath, so often an unhappy ground for Surrey. Now, in the last innings, they had to face the classical slow left-arm bowler, Colin Blythe, on the kind of broken wicket that was supremely his element. In the attempt to save the match, Jack Hobbs batted for almost four hours—Kent won with less than half an hour to spare—for 106 out of a Surrey total of 183. No one else made more than 16; and only three reached double figures. Bill Hitch said of that innings 'To be at the opposite end to Jack that day was blinding; you realised your batting wasn't even the same job. The depressing thing was, he made it look so easy.'

The editor of *Wisden* saw fit, after that season, to include him in his ambiguously designated 'Lord Hawke and Four Cricketers of the Year' in the 1909 *Almanack*. In it, he observed that 'at the present time there is perhaps no better professional batsman in England, except Hayward and Tyldesley.' He said too,

> At first he was rather slow on his feet but now at third man and in the deep field he is almost in the same class as Denton and Tyldesley. In crossing the ball and picking it up he leaves little to be wished for, but he has not Denton's return . . . He is the most likely man among the young professional batsmen to play for England in Test Matches at home in the near future.

That prophecy came true in 1909.

5

The England Player

HIS CRICKET of 1909 ought to have killed Jack Hobbs's superstition about the need for a good start to the season. The Surrey programme began, this time, with a Championship match against Northampton-shire starting on 3 May, when Jack Hobbs scored 12 and 33. Then he galloped away; 205 off Hampshire; 41 and 159 against Warwickshire. To his subsequent regret, he was given the game against Oxford University 'off'; then he made 44 and 4 in the county's first Australian fixture; 160 and 100 against Warwickshire and 99 against Essex up to the first Test.

His form so far in the season had been such that he was bound to be one of the unusually large number of fifteen players summoned to Edgbaston for the first Test. When the question arose as to which of the four to be left out, 'Shrimp' Leveson Gower, a member of the selection committee, pressed Jack Hobbs's case so enthusiastically that Archie MacLaren who afterwards said 'I knew nothing about him then' was persuaded. So Jack Hobbs played in his first home Test; and Tom Hayward was left out.

Australia batted first on a pitch affected by rain and Hirst and Blythe bowled them out for 74. MacLaren took Jack Hobbs in first with him. Whitty bowled the first over; MacLaren played it as a maiden. Charlie Macartney—slow left-arm—opened at the other end

The first of the major partnerships: opening the innings for Surrey with Tom Hayward. Between 1905 and 1914 they shared 40 century opening stands. Lord Dalmeny gave Jack Hobbs his Surrey cap after his first county match when he scored 155 against Essex in May 1905.

The second of the partnerships: with Wilfred Rhodes at Melbourne during the fourth Test of 1911–12, when they scored 323 (in 268 minutes) for the first English wicket against Australia – still the highest opening stand for either country in Tests between them. The two shared 13 century opening stands.

The third partnership: with Andrew Sandham for Surrey. Between 1919 and 1934 they 66 times scored 100 or more for the first wicket; and their 428 against Oxford University in 1926 remains the highest opening stand for Surrey.

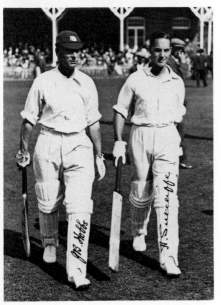

The fourth partnership, generally held to be the finest in all Test cricket: with Herbert Sutcliffe for England. Between 1924 and 1930 they 11 times put on a hundred for the first wicket in Tests; 26 times in all matches.

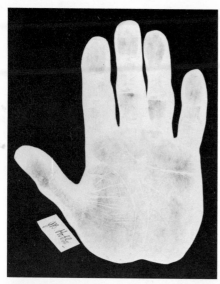

The hand of The Master;
a palm print made in 1925.

The touch of The Master: a leg break from Arthur Mailey placed meticulously between the off-side fieldsmen during The Oval Test of 1926; complete, yet relaxed, control. The wicket-keeper is W. A. Oldfield.

Not too serious;
Jack Hobbs is out;
he has just missed
an attempted big hit
off Greville Stevens
in the Test Trial of 1930.

'Pulling Arthur's leg': he and Arthur Mailey were both of humorous
bent; Jack Hobbs loved to 'pick' his googly and play it through
the leg-side field. He did not always succeed but theirs was invariably
a companionable contest. W. A. Oldfield is keeping wicket;
J. M. Gregory at slip; A. J. Richardson gully.

My dear John, Thank you for your letter. The second week in October would suit me quite well but don't hesitate to change so long as you let me know in good time as I hope to be able to get my wife away for a week during October.

Upon thinking it over I feel notepaper will be better than a card for the few lines of thanks. As usual, you are right and the letter must not be too formal.

After I retired from Surrey I used to motor on Wednesday's, along with my wife to Kimbolton School to give the boys a couple of hours coaching at the nets. We became great friends of the "Head" and his wife and sometimes, when the sun was hot, we would ~~would~~ sit & chat on the cricket ground and let the coaching pass.

In June 1961 Mr. Ingram roped me in for the Father's XI match v the School and in that game I made my last century.

I do not recall playing in any other match after that

All the best,
Yours sincerely
Jack.

The last century recalled, in a letter of 20 September 1962 to the author.

15th. ~~May~~ June, 1963.

23, FURZE CROFT,
FURZE HILL,
HOVE 2, SUSSEX.
TEL: HOVE 34104.

John Arlott Esq.,
    The Old Sun,
        Alresford, Hampshire.

My dear John,
                I am sending you this bat for
young Robert.   When he is old enough to understand
tell him I will give him another when he needs a
larger size.
            May he grow up a keen cricketer & gladden
your heart by making the team of your beloved
Hampshire.   It is unlikely I shall be around to
keep an eye upon him as he grows up, because
of my age and the distance we are apart, so
I beg of you to take my place as well as your
own to see he grows into a Godfearing youth.
            Thank you for everything John.   You have
been very good & kind to me over many years.
            Kindest regards.   Yours sincerely,
                                Jack Hobbs,

Thoughtful to the end; the last time he left Hove, only a few months
before his death, was to attend this boy's christening as a godfather.

In twilight; a study by Tom Blau, 1962.

and Jack Hobbs was lbw to the first ball. He long remembered his disbelief—not at the decision, which he knew was just—but simply that it had happened to him. Few players in the history of the game were more sure of the ball, or less vulnerable at the start of an innings.

Charles Fry, too, was out to his first ball, clean bowled by Macartney; but England contrived a first innings lead of 47. Again Hirst and Blythe bowled out Australia, for 151—Thompson, Rhodes and Jessop, the other three available bowlers, had only five overs in the match—and England needed 105 to win. The pitch was still difficult and the result by no means certain when Charles Fry—also a member of the selection committee—suggested to MacLaren that it would be a psychologically shrewd move to open the innings with the two men who had been out first ball—Jack Hobbs and himself. MacLaren was one of the few England captains likely to accept such an idea; and he did. Together Fry (35 not out) and Hobbs (62 not out) made the runs, at more than a run a minute. Hobbs who, near the end, pulled Macartney for three consecutive and much relished fours, said uncharacteristically 'I played really well—you know when you play well'. *Wisden* noted that 'Fry had only just settled down when the match ended.' Fry himself wrote:

As a spectator at the other crease I have to say that this was as great an innings as I ever saw played by any batsman in any Test match, or any other match. Jack Hobbs on the difficult wicket, took complete charge of the good Australian ' bowling, carted it to every point of the compass, and never made the shred of a mistake. His quickness with his bat and his skill in forcing the direction of his strokes made me feel like a fledgling; and when it comes to it I was not so dusty a driver in those days.

At the finish the crowd swarmed across the ground calling for the English team and especially for Jack Hobbs who, pushed on to the pavilion balcony, waved his cap and backed hastily into the dressing room.

He had now scored 919 runs in seven matches in May—if he had played at Oxford he could well have reached the thousand already—and one playing day of the month remained—the first of the Whitsun Nottingham match at Trent Bridge. In the event, A. O. Jones won the toss, Notts batted all day, and Jack Hobbs never again seriously approached the thousand runs in May.

He did little—with 19 and 9—to help prevent England's defeat in the second Test. In the third he had played himself in securely enough and had made 12 when he pulled Macartney, the ball did not quite reach the boundary and, in starting for a run, he slipped and broke the wicket with his foot. Momentarily he thought he was out and turned to go; but, realising he had completed his stroke first, he appealed to the umpire who said, quite correctly, 'Not out'. At this the Australians—particularly Armstrong—protested, disputing the decision and accusing Jack Hobbs of sharp practice. A man never given to shouting, and certainly not to abuse; he was always distressed by it. He behaved correctly and maintained silence but was so rattled that, all confidence gone, he missed the next straight ball and was bowled. He never forgot, nor forgave, Armstrong for that incident.

In the second innings he was bowled by Cotter for 30 which, to his amazement, proved to be top score of the innings. Before he had towelled off after his bath the remaining seven English wickets—and the match—had been lost to Macartney and Cotter.

Immediately afterwards, in Surrey's match with Lancashire at Old Trafford, Walter Brearley—again—

hit a simple catch to him in the deep: inexplicably, he misjudged it, it landed on the end of a finger and tore off the nail.

The wound was so deep and painful that he did not play for a month; was ruled out of the remaining two Tests and both the Gentlemen-Players matches. He also, less unhappily, missed the dispute about the second Surrey match with the Australians which caused such rifts within the club. As a consequence Jack Crawford ceased to play for the county and went to Australia; Tom Rushby, the main pace bowler, left at the end of the season and went into the Lancashire League; and Alan Marshal was suspended and not re-engaged when his contract ended in the following year. Crawford and Rushby later returned: Marshal did not. Since Hayward, labouring under the handicap of a damaged knee, played in only fourteen Championship matches, Surrey did well to drop only two places in the Championship table.

It was an odd season for Surrey. Owing to an administrative muddle which delighted Jack Hobbs's dry sense of humour, they were scheduled to play two first-class home fixtures—against Lancashire and the return with Oxford University—on the same three days. While the normal team played Lancashire at The Oval, a strange shadow eleven, under John Shuter who had captained the county from 1880 to 1893, lost to the University by an innings and 98 runs at Reigate.

When Jack Hobbs returned to the side after missing seven matches he found it hard to regain his touch and, in twenty innings to the end of the season, he played only four of more than forty. Yet, as a consequence of his fine start, he had the highest aggregate—2114—of the summer. As an augury for the future, the only other batsman to make more than two thousand runs in the season was Wilfred Rhodes.

The second—Lord's—Test of 1909 was the only one in which Jack Hobbs and Tom Hayward played together. They might have done so in at least the third if Hayward had been fully fit. He had, though, turned out at Lord's, against the advice of his doctor, with a damaged and heavily bandaged knee, when they both failed in both innings, putting on 23 and 16 with Hayward 16 and 6; Hobbs 19 and 9.

Hayward, more than ten years the elder of the two, was now thirty-eight; but there had been little deterioration in his powers. In a time of more thinly spread talent he would no doubt have been chosen again; but, as with so many others in that great age, a single failure proved final. Although his batting was less aggressive than it had been six or eight years earlier, even under the handicap of injury, he averaged 41.18 which put him fourth—one place above Jack Hobbs—in the national batting table. He was, too, to regain fitness and form to make 2149 runs in 1911 and to score a thousand each season in eminently sound fashion until the onset of the 1914 War saw the end of his career. He had then scored more runs in first-class cricket than anyone else except W. G. Grace.

His partnership with Jack Hobbs was of infinite benefit to the younger man, who was always happy to acknowledge the fact. To observe the best professional batsman of the day from the opposite crease must be a privilege for anyone with the perception to learn from his precept. It was generally assumed that, while many of Jack Hobbs's wide batting powers stemmed from innate talent, his defence which, at the pinch, was superlative—especially on the back foot—was based on the method of Tom Hayward.

They were the greatest opening pair the game had known until their time. They shared forty opening stands of over a hundred, more than twice as many as the Yorkshire pair, Brown and Tunnicliffe, who, of course, set the long standing record of 554 in 1898. In the period before the First World War they were approached only by Fry and Vine of Sussex with thirty-three and Jones and Iremonger of Nottinghamshire with twenty-four. Much of the strength of their pairing lay in the ability to suit their play to the state of the match, wicket or opposition. While they were both fundamentally sound in defence, they both had a wide range of attacking strokes which made them difficult not merely to dominate, but even to contain. The bond between the two men was strong, but completely undemonstrative. Jack Hobbs never shook off the feeling of being the Cambridge lad looking up to the great man; and his respect for Tom Hayward never faded. It would have given them and, no doubt, many other Cambridge people, profound pleasure to have had a successful partnership in a Test.

Jack Hobbs was an automatic choice for the team to go to South Africa in the following winter. In 1905–06 South Africa had reached a new peak of achievement when, largely through their googly bowlers, they took the series by four Tests to one against an England side which, if not of full strength, was at least a good second eleven. They had, too, played well in losing the three match rubber of 1907 in England by the only Test finished, but taking a strong position in the third.

Only a powerful English team had any hope of winning; but selection was to some extent hampered by the South African insistence—usually presumed to be for economic reasons—on a large proportion of amateurs, at a time when many of those who stood highest in the English team were not able to leave the country for an entire winter.

In the event the party, though certainly not without

talent, contained only three first choices of the preceding summer's Tests with Australia. By comparison with the teams fielded in those matches, there were significant absentees in the 'four' who had not accepted terms for Australia—George Hirst, Johnny Tyldesley, Tom Hayward and Dick Lilley—C. B. Fry, Reggie Spooner, Kenneth Hutchings, Gilbert Jessop, Archie MacLaren, Pelham Warner and, most significant of all in view of his performances in South Africa on the matting wickets there in 1913–14, S. F. Barnes, then, as for many years, arguably the best bowler in the world. *Wisden* described it as:

a good although by no means representative side . . . the weak point was a lack of class and stability in the batting . . . among the fourteen players only Hobbs would at home have been sure of his place in a Test Match for batting alone.

The team did well to lose the rubber by only three matches to two; but there were few personal successes. Simpson-Hayward, the lob bowler, performed outstandingly; Blythe, in the two Tests when he played, and George Thompson well; Claude Buckenham faithfully. The batsmen though—with Jack Hobbs as the solitary and glorious exception—could not cope with the googly bowling of Faulkner and Vogler, who took sixty-five wickets between them. This tour established Jack Hobbs as a senior English cricketer; and the best player of googly bowling in the world; and it saw the founding of the historic opening partnership of Hobbs and Rhodes.

The extent of Jack Hobbs's stature in this series is indicated by figures: his Test average, 67, 37, was twice that of the next English batsman George Thompson, with 33.37. Wilfred Rhodes was at this point—or at

least against the googly bowlers—an assistant rather
than a fully-fledged partner; his figure was 25.11. It is
even more indicative of the character and quality of
Jack Hobbs as a cricketer that, in all matches—a
number were played against local fifteens or sixteens—
his average was 58.81; in the keener competition of
eleven-a-side games (including Tests) 62.84; in Tests
alone 67.37. The sharpest opposition invariably evoked
from him the most competitive performance.

His only previous experience of the South African
googly bowling was in 1907. Although he was not then
a member of the English team, he played against them
for Surrey, when he scored 18 and 41; and for C. I.
Thornton's XI when he made 78 and—out at the start
to the fast bowler, Kotze—5. This, though, was his
first experience of matting wickets. He moved at once
into touch with 110 in his first innings—against
Sixteen Western Province Colts—then 114 against the
full Western Province side. In the first Test, which
England lost as narrowly as by 19 runs, when all twenty
wickets fell to the googly bowling of Vogler and
Faulkner, Jack Hobbs's 89 was top score in the first
innings—when he and Wilfred Rhodes shared an
opening partnership of 159—his 35 highest but one of
the second innings.

On this tour, in their first partnership, Hobbs and
Rhodes first employed their method of running quick
singles without calling. In the first Test at Johannesburg, S. J. Snooke, a tall fast-medium bowler, was
lifting awkwardly off the mat. Between overs they
decided to take a short run off his first ball; Jack Hobbs
played a dead bat stroke, the ball rolled towards silly
point and, before a fieldsman had moved, they had
taken a single. They did the same for a few more overs
against Snooke, who was completely unsettled and
taken off early: and they continued to employ the tactic.

Jack Hobbs and Wilfred Rhodes had immense respect for one another. At this stage Wilfred Rhodes had not yet completed his remarkable advance from a slow bowler who went in last for England, to an established Test opening batsman. He was a shrewd batsman, basically correct; safe in defence, and a cold punisher of the bad ball. Jack always thought him the best runner of all his partners:

> Wilfred would always come . . . he wasn't a sprinter, but he was always backing up a yard or two and we knew each other so well that, just a nod—or nothing at all—we went. You could say he ran better for me than I did for him because, while I often started almost before I had finished my stroke, he was not so quickly away; but we hardly ever had a run out. We trusted each other completely. You wouldn't call Wilfred a great batsman—not as good as Tom Hayward or Herbert Sutcliffe; but he was so sound; he never attempted anything he couldn't do; the other side had to get him out.

Immediately after the first Test, in the match against Natal, the pair had an opening of 207, of which Rhodes made 64; Hobbs 163 in 155 minutes. In the second Test they started off with 94 and 48; Hobbs with 53, and 70 out of 106 in seventy-five minutes, was top scorer in both innings. South Africa won by 95 runs. In the third Test, he caught sunstroke while fielding, batted at number seven in the first innings and made only 11. In the second, still not fit, he went in at 42 for three (the fourth wicket fell at the same figure) and effectively decided the match—which England won by three wickets—with 93 not out, substantially the highest score of an innings in which no one else made more than 45. The fourth was his only failure of the series; and he was not alone. Of the first three English batsmen, he made 1 and 0—by far his worst Test performance—

Rhodes 0 and 5; David Denton 0 and 10. South Africa took the match—and the rubber with it—by four wickets. Finally, at Cape Town, Jack Hobbs scored his first Test century—187 in 225 minutes—and dominated a new Test record for a first wicket partnership of 221 with Wilfred Rhodes, who made 77. Syd Gregory who was shortly to become captain of Australia and as a typical Australian cricketer, was not given to flattering his opponents, watched that Cape Town match and gave as his opinion 'I believe Hobbs to be just about the finest bat in the world today'. *Wisden* was moved to superlatives—

> Beyond everything else from the English point of view the feature of the tour was the superb batting of Hobbs, who easily adapted himself to the matting wickets and scored from the famous googly bowlers with amazing skill and facility. When they came home the other members of the team could not say too much in his praise. Leveson Gower, in his captain's report, wrote 'Without question the feature of the tour was the batting of Hobbs. I have never seen better either in England or anywhere else.'

On that tour he 'discovered' googly bowling. His basic method was the classic one—to push forward to the ball that could be smothered; otherwise, to go as far back as possible and play it off the pitch. That method is not so simple as it may sound because it involves the ability to judge exactly the length of the ball early in flight; and, against wrist spin with its mixture of dip, tendency to float on, or drift away, Jack Hobbs's unfailing ability to estimate the point of pitch was a rare and essential gift. Undoubtedly he developed an instinctive identification of the leg break and googly, sensing—and at times actually seeing—the spin on the ball. For most of the latter half of his career he was content that there was no googly bowler he could not

'pick'. On the other hand, Tom Hayward, handi-
capped by increasing weight and lack of mobility—'I
think I am batting as well as ever but my legs are not
what they used to be'—became highly vulnerable to the
googly. Despite his success against the South Africans
in England in 1907, he became extremely sensitive
about this weakness, the more so because his young
partner played it as a strength.

This gave poignancy to a story Jack Hobbs—as he
never minded doing—used to tell against himself.
Lockhart, the extremely slow Cambridge University
wrist spinner, bowled him a ball which he identified as a
googly and moved across to hit it on the legside; then,
remembering the two deep fieldsmen there, he decided
to take it on the pads; instead, it turned, so sharply as
to bowl him behind his legs. Thereupon, Tom Hayward in the pavilion, said, with a great laugh, 'Jack is
showing us how to play the googly'.

Jack long maintained that the eighteen months of
almost continuous cricket entailed by an overseas tour
between English seasons took much of the zest and
pleasure out of the game; and he was at less than his
best in 1910. Although he scored 1982 runs it was, in
some ways, the worst season of his mature career; after
the matting of South Africa the wickets of a wet
English summer seemed strange; he never truly found
touch.

Again in 1911 his figures hardly reflected his reputation or his ability. He made 2376 runs but, far too
often, he played himself in, only to be out for something
between 40 and 70. Perhaps he relaxed for lack of high
competition: this was the second consecutive English
season without a Test series. Certainly he responded
splendidly to one challenge. He was chosen for both
Gentlemen-Players matches but after he failed at The
Oval with 12 and 38 and was clearly in a bad patch, it

was suggested that he might stand down from the
Lord's fixture. His responses were characteristic: in
the first place he courteously agreed to stand down—
because there were so many fine players available—in
the second, when MCC decided to stand by their
original selection, he batted as well as he—or anyone
else—did in that entire season.

This had all the ingredients of an outstanding Hobbs
performance. He had scored only 18 in the first
innings; in the second, his side—needing 423 in less
than five hours—was in a losing position. The pitch
was difficult. It had never played well from the start of
the game; it was quite fast but not true, and now it was
at its most difficult. The bowling of Frank Foster—fast
left-arm—W. B. Burns, extremely fast right-arm; John
Douglas, fast-medium swing; and P. R. le Couteur, leg-
breaks and googlies, was varied and hostile. The game
and the clock were both running strongly for the
bowlers. The recognised bad-wicket master, Johnny
Tyldesley, made 41: Tom Hayward, in his last Gentlemen *v* Players, 35: otherwise the batting crumbled
round him. In those circumstances he contrived to play
such attacking cricket as to carry his bat for 154, made
in three-and-a-quarter hours, out of a total of 292.

There was never any doubt of his selection for the
1911–12 tour of Australia. The party was strong but,
again, not the strongest possible. Two of the first three
batsmen in the national averages were not available.
They were C. B. Fry—first, a lordly 17 ahead of the
next man—and Reggie Spooner, third: those two, in
the absence of Hobbs, unfit, opened the innings for
England against the Rest in the Test trial. Otherwise,
apart from Jessop and Fane, the selectors had their
wish.

The team that eventually sailed under Pelham
Warner—who, through illness, did not play after the

opening match of the tour—was a procession of historic cricketing names: John Douglas (vice-captain, who took over for all Tests), Frank Foster, Wilfred Rhodes, Sydney Barnes, Jack Hobbs, George Gunn, Herbert Strudwick, Sep Kinneir, Joe Vine, Jim Iremonger, Frank Woolley, Philip Mead, 'Tiger' Smith, 'Young Jack' Hearne and Bill Hitch. They proved outstandingly successful. After losing the first Test, they won the next four, largely through the pace bowling of Frank Foster and Sydney Barnes, who between them took 66 wickets in the series at about 22 each. Of all English sides, until Brearley's in 1978–79, only Percy Chapman's in 1928–29 and Douglas Jardine's of 1932–33 have ever done so well in Australia. The batting was dominated by Hobbs. The Australian bowling was strong: Cotter still commanded high pace: Doctor Hordern was at his finest as a googly bowler— he took 32 wickets in the rubber, including that of Hobbs four times; Macartney was a valuable left-arm bowler; Kelleway tight at medium pace; and Armstrong an astute leg-spinner. Against that opposition, Jack Hobbs's Test scores were 63, 22; 6, 126 not out; 187, 3; 178; 32 and 45. His opening of 323 with Wilfred Rhodes at Melbourne was at that time the highest stand for any wicket in Tests between England and Australia; and, to their enduring pleasure in recollection, it took only four-and-a-half hours. On this tour their opening partnership reached its peak. In Tests they put on 45, 29; 10, 57; 147, 5; 323; 15 and 76. Once again Jack Hobbs's capacity for producing his best in face of the sternest competition was reflected in his figures; in all matches (including Tests) he averaged 55.04; in Tests only, 82.75. The significance of such figures is relative; but his average was 24 ahead of the next English batsman—who was Wilfred Rhodes—and 46 more than the leading Australian, Syd Gregory, who thus saw his South African assessment confirmed. That tour, too, cemented Jack's long friendship with Bert Strudwick who was at that time his landlord and next-door neighbour. They had great respect for one another's ability and they were deeply loyal and uncomplicated friends for more than fifty years.

Back in England in 1912, he was top of the English averages in the Triangular Tournament against Australia and South Africa. Against Australia he began with a century at Lord's; made only 19 in his single innings at Old Trafford but 66, highest score of the first innings, on a bad wicket in the decisive match at The Oval. In the South African games he failed at Lord's; made a superb 50 in an hour at Headingley and 68—by 26 the highest score of the match on either side—to settle the Oval Test.

In the two Gentlemen-Players matches he was at his imperious best. At The Oval he scored a duck in the first innings, in the second, almost predictably, he went in with Wilfred Rhodes and scored 50 out of 56 in twenty-one minutes. At Lord's his 94 was the highest score of the match; *Wisden* commented that he 'was almost reckless in the later part of his innings'. In another part of the *Almanack* it was observed that he 'played much finer cricket for England than for his county'; and Surrey fell to seventh position in the table.

In 1913 he stepped up to his full eminence. He scored 2238 runs in Surrey's Championship matches alone—878—more than the county's next man, who was Ernie Hayes—altogether, 2605 (at 50.09) with nine centuries. *Wisden* referred to him as 'not only the best bat in Surrey but by general consent the best in England'. In the winter of 1913–14 he went again to South Africa, under John Douglas in a side which won the rubber by four matches to one. Although he did not score a century in Tests, he was out clear at the top of the averages for all matches and of both sides in Tests. In putting England safe from defeat in the one Test they did not win, he made 97 in 135 minutes.

This aggressive freedom of strokeplay was now linked with consistency. Once again he returned somewhat weary from an overseas tour; and early in the 1914 season he struck a bad patch. He resolved to hit his way out of it against, of all counties, Yorkshire. Their bowlers were George Hirst, Major Booth, Alonzo Drake, Wilfred Rhodes and Roy Kilner; four Test players, the fifth their most successful bowler of the season. On a soft Bradford wicket Jack Hobbs scored exactly a hundred, without a mistake, in an hour-and-a-quarter; with five sixes—two in an over from Wilfred Rhodes—and eleven fours. In the second innings he effectively won the match with 74 in an hour-and-a-quarter; one six off Alonzo Drake smashed the face of the clock on the football stand. No one else made more than 21 in the innings; and Surrey won narrowly by 28 runs. From then until the end of the season he could hardly do wrong. For the Players against Gentlemen at The Oval he made a faultless 156—twice as many as any other score in the match. That was one of eleven centuries in a season's aggregate of 2697, 221 ahead of anyone else's. He effectively took the Championship to Surrey. In match after match he was top scorer and his rate was high: his 183 against Warwickshire, for instance, was made—without a mistake—in 170 minutes. He had a second long score against Yorkshire at Lord's in a match rearranged when The Oval was requisitioned by the Army: he made 202 in 220 minutes and, in the last match, 141 at almost a run a minute against Gloucestershire. Many of these innings, too, were faultless. As *Wisden* remarked 'Hobbs stood out by himself—pre-eminently the batsman of the season.'

This was the high peak of his cricket. No one can guess, and he himself never surmised, what he might have achieved in the next four years if they had not been given to a graver and more evil matter than cricket. Nevertheless he was already good enough for one of the sternest and most penetrative judges of the game to call him 'The Perfect Batsman'.

He commanded, and played, all the strokes used, except in mischief, always to the right ball. Asked once if he had a favourite stroke, he said 'I always liked it to be the right one' and, with a broad grin, 'especially if it went for four.'

6

The Splendid Peak

WHEN the First World War broke out, Jack Hobbs, rising thirty-two years old, was, beyond question, the finest batsman in the world. His face was sensitive; steady grey eyes set in a network of wrinkles engraved by sunshine and laughter. The cartoonists picked on a slightly long nose as a characteristic for exaggeration; but it was quizzical rather than large. He had put on muscle since his gawky days in Cambridge and now combined both the stamina and the litheness of the well-trained athlete. He had strong but whippy wrists and the loose shoulders of the free batsman. Five-feet-nine tall, trim and well proportioned, he weighed a little under eleven and a half stone; because he always kept himself meticulously fit, his weight varied only by about half a stone to the end of his playing days. An impressive cricketing appearance was heightened by turn-out immaculate to the sharp edge between blanco and polished edge of boot-sole.

His stance at the wicket was relaxed, sideways-on, perfectly balanced on neat feet. Many batsmen give some indication by their position as to whether they are initially prepared to play forward or back. Jack Hobbs did not; he was poised, feet rather closer together than is the case with most batsmen, ready to go either forward or back as he judged. Perhaps, indeed, of all his batting gifts, his capacity for making that decision was the most outstanding. He once said 'I think far more people are out through playing back when they should play forward, or forward when they should play back, than for any other reason.' He made that mistake more rarely than most. His footwork—of which other fine batsmen spoke with something near awe—enabled him to capitalise on that instinctive judgement: and it was so fast that he frequently dictated length by his speed of movement. Like most batsmen, as he grew older, he tended, increasingly, to play back—'giving myself more time to see it'—but in his prime he really seemed to have no preference. (W. G. Grace, incidentally, tended in his old age to play forward more than formerly.)

He held the bat in the middle of the handle with his right hand, the index finger of the left touching it. Unlike many batsmen—and contrary to the advice of most coaches anxious to avoid or correct 'too much bottom hand'—he gripped firmly with his right hand, a little more loosely with the left to allow full freedom of the wrists. The consequent scope of movement gave him the widest possible range of strokes; he had them all; and he used them all. Nothing is so disconcerting for a bowler as to have one ball driven 'over the top' and the next cut for four. When he decided to go out to drive he would often leap far down the pitch, uninhibited by fear of being stumped. When he played back he did so with certainty, often very close indeed to the wicket.

He was, too, a 'touch' player; capable of 'checking' a stroke which, struck with normal force would have reached a fieldsman too quickly to allow a run to be taken. Especially as he matured, he developed this technique to a high degree, playing the ball slowly to the fieldsman to give more time for the single. He excelled, too, in placing; and seemed at times with mischievous delight, to find gaps in a captain's carefully set field; and often as soon as one was plugged, he would puckishly hit through the position from which the fieldsman had been taken.

Placing was, too, an essential ingredient of his almost uncanny ability to take a single off virtually any ball he wished. The other ingredients were control, and his splendid running between wickets, which demonstrated the truth of the old adage in cricket 'more runs are missed than made'. Tom Hayward was in some ways a staid man; not inclined to scamper quick runs; and Jack would never have assumed with him such dominance over calling and running as he exerted in his partnerships with Wilfred Rhodes, Herbert Sutcliffe and Andrew Sandham. The first stride of the run seemed to be part of his stroke and he never doubted the response. In each pairing the understanding and the trust were complete; the ball would be pushed away barely clear—or short—of a fieldsman; a nod, or even nothing, and they were gone.

Jack Hobbs had, too, a mental filing system for opponents; he knew every heavy-footed, uncoordinated or slow reacting fieldsman and he would surely seek him out and exploit his weakness. He was fond of playing the ball to the right of a bowler pulling away to the off side; there was invariably a run to be had before he could twist back. Again and again when no run seemed possible, they would finish their single at a walk. Oddly enough, none of those players—not even Sutcliffe with Holmes—took anything approaching the same number of quick runs with any other partner.

It was all part of a considered strategic pattern to take the initiative from the fielding side; the bowler hesitating about pulling away as far as usual in hope of trapping the batsman into a run-out; the captain bringing his fieldsmen up a yard or two to prevent the push-and-run tactic, only for a four to be hit past a man too close in to stop it. Some players became rattled under the pressure, and in face of the ridicule of the crowd; for the quick run—'pulling fat bacon'—is always good for a laugh.

Jack Hobbs employed his range of stroke-making often, too, for tactical purposes. He would rout a bowler who could not take punishment by attacking him: or against one bowling well, defend so soundly and apparently easily that he was taken off, disheartened. Tom Goddard used to relate how, often, when Gloucester were bowling on a turning wicket, Jack Hobbs would launch an attack on Charlie Parker, a left-arm bowler who spun the ball considerably.

> I have seen him hit Charlie over the top of extra cover or mid-off four or five times in a couple of overs and drive him off. Then, for the next hour or two, Charlie was fielding at third man when he should have been bowling Surrey out; but instead of that, Jack was making a hundred.

His batting was interwoven with an instinctive comprehension of the bowled ball; he felt for it, often harnessed its spin or pace to his stroke. Len Hutton much resembled him in this sensitivity. He was so sure of the ball that he could often play an incorrect stroke for tactical purposes. He would pull a leg-break or slow left-arm bowler against the spin through the leg side to break up a packed off-side field so that he could make runs through the openings that were left.

Much of his certainty stemmed from the fact that he was so correct in method—the sideways-on approach, high right hand, long, full straight swing—that he was always presenting the largest possible area of bat-surface to the ball. This enabled him to drive the perfect length ball with relatively little risk, yet another tactical advantage against even the best bowlers.

J. N.—Jack—Crawford, often said to have been the finest of all schoolboy cricketers, played for Surrey during Jack Hobbs's first five years with the county. Then Crawford had a disagreement with the club, left and went to Australia and did not return to them until 1919. That meant that in subsequent years he was able to make a comparative assessment of the young Hobbs and the established Test player.

Usually when you see a talented but inexperienced young batsman you wonder what he has to learn before he gets his game right. With Jack Hobbs you never felt that. He seemed a complete player from the start—without a real flaw, but perhaps in those early years he got himself out trying to do too much; and, at times, through worrying when he had no need to worry. When he came to Australia in 1911–12, though, he was a far more mature, confident—almost assertive—batsman. You could say that he simply did not have a weakness. He was never off balance; and he was so quick without ever having to hurry. He seemed to flow through his strokes; yet he sometimes left a ball so late that you thought it was through, when he hit it for four.

In his own words:

Perhaps I was cocky; but I don't think I was—not like that. I never said anything about my batting; but there is no doubt, when I was young, I thought I could do it all— and I tried to. You see I enjoyed it so much and I was making runs all the time—and that was my living. I never took such risks after the war because I didn't feel I could.

In 1914 A. C. MacLaren, the former Lancashire and England Captain, commissioned Cherry Kearton Limited, the firm of early documentary film-makers, to film Jack Hobbs playing a series of strokes. He batted on a true Oval pitch against two bowlers as good and as different as the South African leg spinner, Syd Pegler, and Bill Hitch of Surrey, then about as fast as anyone in England. MacLaren was an orthodox—even classical— batsman in method; a Test selector and an astute analyst of technique. From the series of shots of Hobbs, he selected ninety-eight, illustrating ten strokes —a drive to mid-off; a cover drive; two of changes from attack to defence; a square cut; a square drive; a high off-drive; a drive to the right of cover point; a high straight drive; and playing a ball off the left knee in front of square leg.

They were reproduced, with analytical and elucidatory text by MacLaren, in a book which he titled *The Perfect Batsman* (Cassell, 1926). The attacking strokes are marked by a high, wristy backlift, uninhibited footwork, perfect flow and generous follow-through; the two changes, by rapid yet orderly adjustment.

MacLaren was generally a severe critic; therefore, when he traffics in superlatives, the praise is high. He remarks 'Everything that Hobbs does as a batsman or fieldsman is without fuss, and graceful. He has never departed from sound methods, but has kept his natural free game pure throughout his career.' At another point he asserts 'It is essential to use one's brain well, and this Hobbs has always done; I never recollect him being sent back to the pavilion having played the wrong game for the occasion.'

It was as characteristic of Jack Hobbs as it is generally rare, that, in his later days he never compared the players of older generations unfavourably with those of his own time. Few outstanding people in any field are clear-minded, generous or strong-willed enough to observe that rule of behaviour. On the other hand, he consistently made the point that he scored his runs under the 'old' lbw law by which a batsman could only be out leg-before-wicket to a ball pitching in the straight line of wicket-to-wicket. It is probable that the introduction of the 'new' lbw law was the most far-reaching reform made in the laws since the legalisation of over-arm bowling; certainly it altered the balance between batsman and bowler more profoundly than any other single piece of legislation for seventy years. Introduced experimentally in 1935, and incorporated into the laws in 1937, it made it possible for a batsman to be out lbw to a ball pitching outside the off stump, provided the ball would have hit the stumps, and that the part of his body struck was in the straight line between wicket and wicket. Previously a batsman could, with impunity, play the sharpest off break with his pad—provided it pitched outside the off stump. The batsmen of the pre-1935 era did simply that. Thus, for some two centuries, many of the finest break-backs ever bowled simply thumped unavailingly against a leg or an out-thrust pad. Like all good sticky wicket players, Jack Hobbs frequently played off-spinners on a turning wicket with his pads—he did so against Arthur Richardson in the historic and decisive fifth Test of 1926. His judgement of the pitch of the ball and his feeling for the position of his stumps were such that he could work to inches in padding up: and his standing was such that he was unlikely to be given a bad decision. No batsman of that period—certainly none of the top rank—failed to take advantage of the old law. It would have been strange if they had, since it was not regarded as unfair; it had never been otherwise. The law simply gave them the right to defend their stumps with their legs against the turning or swinging ball. Indeed, some profound and informed cricket thinkers believe that a reversion to the 'old' law would be beneficial to the general health and standard of the game. Ranji and

Charles Fry, in their different ways, were brilliant players; but they both played the dangerous-looking off-break—when it pitched outside the off stump—with their pads as a matter of course. Indeed, during the nineteen-twenties and nineteen-thirties a substantial school of thought seemed to regard pad play almost as a separate facet of the art of batting. That preoccupation eventually led to the introduction of the new law. Jack Hobbs recognised that it made batting more difficult than in his day. There can be no doubt that he would have been as fine a batsman by comparison with his contemporaries under the new law as under the old. He solved every problem bowlers ever posed to him. There is, too, every reason to believe that his considerable skill in playing the ball that moved into him, and his controlled power on the leg side would have found him outstandingly equipped to deal with the changed situation—perhaps to his comparative advantage. Nevertheless, pad play—so long as the point of pitch is correctly identified—must always be less dangerous than playing with the bat. The size and the rate of his scoring allow no suggestion that Jack Hobbs was a slavish pad player; he was simply a batsman of his age who batted in accordance with the laws of his age.

By 1914 he had become the finest cover point in the game. A shrewd tactician, varying his depth and angle as he judged, he worked to lure batsmen into the belief that there was a single to him. Then his immense acceleration would take him to the ball extremely quickly, his pick-up merged with the whip back of his arm; the throw, from stooping shoulder-level, used to hit Bert Strudwick's gloves—or the bails—with a crack like a stockwhip. Pelham Warner, in his report on the Australian tour of 1911–12, wrote:

In Hobbs we had a cover point the equal of any fieldsman in that position I have ever seen. Not even G. L. Jessop at his best is his superior. I have never seen a cover point hit the wicket so often. During the tour he ran out no less than fifteen men.

To his amusement, too, he was top of the bowling averages for that tour with five wickets at 18.00. He put out Collins, Kelleway, Barbour and J. D. Scott for 25 in the second New South Wales match after the regular bowlers had been heavily punished in an innings of 403. He bowled from a high action, at medium pace, with the nip of the natural bowler, and a stock-in-trade largely of outswingers, but with the ability occasionally to make one move back off the seam. Several shrewd judges thought his gifts such that, if he had not devoted so much attention—and, crucially, energy—to batting, he might have made a distinguished career as a bowler. In 1911, against a capable Oxford University batting side in The Parks, he bowled throughout their second innings, 26 overs, and, despite having five catches dropped in the slips, took seven wickets—including the first five—for 56. It was a humid day and the ball swung violently and late in the still air. His best bowling, though, was in 1920, in a match with War-wickshire at Birmingham when Tom Rushby sent one of his notorious telegrams and did not arrive. Jack Hobbs opened the bowling with Hitch, at that time England's fast bowler, and who was given choice of ends. He took no wickets, but Hobbs, making the ball bite back sharply off a slow pitch, took five—including the first four batsmen—for 21.

War ended the 1914 season; and caused the Surrey-Kent match, which would have been Jack Hobbs's benefit, to be transferred to Lord's. The result was disappointing and he was happy to accept the Surrey

Club's offer to allow them to keep the gate money and defer his benefit until after the war. Initially he worked in a munitions factory, until he joined the Royal Flying Corps in 1916. Up to that point he had played some cricket in the Bradford League where, for the only time, he batted against S. F. Barnes, and scored—according to Barnes—a chanceless century. That remains a hint of what he might have done in those four lost years.

7

The High Plateau

IT WAS Jack Hobbs's habit to say, calmly and quietly, 'I was never half the player after the first war that I was before.' It is probable, too, that he was never finer than in 1914. Those who watched him in 1919 and 1920, however, thought him still a truly great, free, batsman then. He would say, if questioned, that his thigh muscle injury and appendicitis in 1921 probably had a greater effect on him than the War gap, and hampered his batting for some three years afterwards. By then he was into his forties and many of the strokes of five years before—1919, not 1914—were no longer 'business'. Nevertheless, in all the years from 1919 until 1933 (the season before his retirement, when he averaged 61) he scored quite prolifically.

MacLaren wrote in 1926 'In spite of all the hundreds he has made recently, he had more strokes in 1914 than he has now, owing to his wisdom in only attempting now what his years will allow him.' He scored 35,017 runs in those fifteen post-war years: and in only one season or tour—1923 (37.78)—was his average below 51; eight times it was over 60. In that period, too, he made 131 of his 197 centuries.

The fact is that, for those amazing fifteen years after he was thirty-six, he was, apart from Bradman, the most consistently heavy run-scorer the game has ever known. Unlike Bradman, though, he scored his runs in

all conditions. The best judges—including himself—
declared that he was a lesser batsman than in the years
to 1914; and one who did not see him in that earlier
period cannot quibble with that decision; but he can
say that the Jack Hobbs of post-1925 was still a superb
batsman. His eminence at this time—indeed, for his
entire passage along his high plateau—lay in his ability
to make runs against all kinds of bowling on all types of
wickets.

Once, taxed with the question 'Would it be true to
say that during the 'twenties you could have made a
century almost whenever you wanted?', he merely
chuckled. Pressed—'Please, be serious'—he said, gravely
enough

> No one could make a century every time he went in; no
> one has enough strength for that; but it is true that I made
> hundreds more frequently then than I had done before.
> You see, the bowling wasn't as good as it was before the
> War, it really wasn't. Some of the counties were very little
> trouble. You must remember, too, that we played half
> our matches at the Oval and you couldn't have had a
> better wicket than the Oval in the twenties. Well, Andy
> and I would go in and, if we got going well—say we had
> about seventy or eighty a bit before one o'clock—and the
> best of the bowling was not so sharp; well, you had to
> remember, Surrey had a lot of batting in those days.
> There was Tom Shepherd, Andy Ducat, Mr Jardine [he
> called all amateurs 'Mister' to the end of his days], Mr
> Jeacocke, Mr Fender, Bob Gregory, as well as Andy. So
> you'd have a bit of a hit; against one of your old pals; you
> know, the chaps who did the real work, like George
> Geary, Alec Kennedy, Jack Newman, Jack Mercer, Jack
> Durston, or Fred Root. Sometimes it went wrong and
> they weren't very pleased with you: you didn't get out
> and, before you knew where you were, you'd got a
> hundred. But more often—they were good bowlers, those
> chaps—you would be out for about sixty or so and the

others could come in, and we'd have a fair score by the end of the day. There were other times, though; say Sandy went early or we were on a difficult pitch or someone—like Maurice Tate, say, or Ted McDonald, or Harold Larwood—was bowling really well; that was the time you had to earn your living. After all, Surrey paid me to make runs; not just runs when we didn't need them, but runs when we did need them. So that was the time when you had to knuckle down to it and make a hundred if you could. Often you couldn't, but you'd make as many as you could. I would have said against some counties then, on a good pitch, you could have backed yourself to make a hundred if you wanted. To tell you the truth, centuries never bothered me; nor records really; nor averages. It always seemed to me that cricket would be a better game if the papers didn't publish the averages. It didn't bother me if I didn't get a century; but, you see, it used to bother my friends; they thought it was important; so, often, you used to think, well, it will make them happy, and you would go on. Of course I was earning my living; but it was batting I enjoyed—batting and everything that goes with it, like working out what the bowler is up to; or trying to break up his field; or collaring him: or keeping him out; or hanging on until the pitch got easier. I can say I always did enjoy it until, at the end, my legs got so tired. Even then I might have gone on, but I had had a long run—much longer than players nowadays—and it wouldn't have been fair to the younger men, especially since I couldn't play the full six days a week all the season.

When the 1914 War ended, though, he returned to cricket with hungry enthusiasm. There was never anything else for him in terms of pleasure. Other matters, however, concerned him more gravely. He was a married man with four growing children and, for five years, in common with most men who served in that war, he had earned little to make any significant contribution towards his family's future or security.

Jack Hobbs was a thrifty man. That is not to say he was mean; he was extremely generous, as those he loved and some unfortunates of his acquaintance, would testify. He cared for money, not as money, but as a safeguard against the kind of poverty he had experienced in his childhood and against which he so carefully shielded his children.

His long deferred benefit—the last fixture of 1919 at The Oval—proved historic. The subscription lists had been left open since 1914, and the result was described by *Wisden* as 'a big success, the net sum given to Hobbs being £1671.2s.7d.' By modern standards that seems a pitiful sum; but it gave Jack Hobbs his first opportunity of a measurable income outside cricket. He had been offered a coaching engagement in South Africa for the winter of 1919-20 at a figure which would have shown a profit. He considered the matter sagely; decided against the South African offer, and invested virtually all he had in a sports goods shop. It was at No. 59 Fleet Street, next door to the little—but, as nostalgia recalls, friendly and well-tabled—Wellington Restaurant. It remained there for fifty years, the unchanged lettering of its sign 'JACK HOBBS LTD' changing in impact, with the passing of time, from the brightly fashionable to the pleasantly period.

Every shopping day out of the cricket season and, later, almost until his death, on at least two days a week, any potential customer could ask for—and be served by—Jack Hobbs himself. He had had no experience at all of keeping a shop; nor, indeed, of any kind of commerce. He taught himself to keep the books; signed all the cheques and, even in his old age, supervised its affairs by two visits a week. It was an honest business. He had no wish to make slick money, but to carry on an honest trade. Because he was Jack Hobbs, many people came to his shop to buy once: that was to be expected: success lay in their reactions. Because they were treated with courtesy; because the prices were fair and the quality of the goods sound, they returned. So he established a business which made him and his eldest son an extremely good living and kept them and a staff of some five or six busy.

Lately, after fifty years, 'young Jack' moved it to Islington where it continued to flourish. His father was not the first cricketer to take that course. Arthur Shrewsbury, Alfred Shaw, William Gunn, Frank Sugg—batsmen all, be it noted—had gone prosperously ahead of him. They, though, were north-countrymen, independent, and players for counties less feudal than those of the south. As soon as his shop prospered—which was almost at once—he stood in a changed position. He was a professional cricketer who earnt more from another source than from cricket. There was no thought in his mind of giving up playing cricket; but he was sufficiently financially independent to have stood upon his dignity at any point of his dealings with the Surrey Club. It never occurred to him to do so; and, such was his eminence, as a batsman alone, that the situation never arose. It was, though, understood that he was not dependent upon the club— as all his colleagues, except the telegram-happy Tom Rushby, were—for his basic bread and butter. This simple fact—and it could hardly be more simple—was a major step in the elevation of the professional cricketer—indeed, the professional games player in Britain—above dependence.

Some of his contemporaries regarded him with doubt, if not disapproval. They felt that, by his success, he was setting himself above them. In fact, by improving his own standing he was lifting that of all professional cricketers. For instance, he took his wife on overseas tours. There were some official doubts on grounds of 'discipline' and, had he been a lesser batsman, he might have found the matter more difficult. Wives had followed touring teams before, if not with the official party, at least, they had been near at hand, in the same country and the same towns; but they had been wives of amateurs. Jack Hobbs was a devoted family man; he refused several overseas tours simply because he preferred to be at home with his wife and children. For that reason he never went to the West Indies or India; and he turned down the 1922–23 tour to South Africa. Indeed, although he gave no reason, he originally refused the invitation to go to Australia in 1924–25 on purely domestic grounds. In the same winter a private team, captained by the Hon. Lionel Tennyson and subsidised by 'Solly' Joel, was to tour South Africa, and Jack Hobbs was asked to join it, with the inducement that his wife could accompany him, with all her expenses paid. When Lord's—in the mighty person of Lord Harris—heard that he was considering the offer, he was told that he might take his wife on MCC's Australian tour—provided that he paid all her expenses. He demurred—characteristically—on the grounds that he would not be responsible for another player being put out of the Australian party; eventually he was taken as an 'extra' player; his wife went with him and he happily paid for her. Once more, in his quietly determined fashion, he had achieved his end. His Test average of 63 rendered the bargain sound.

Sydney Barnes held similar basic views. He thought professional cricketers were underpaid; and that wives should be allowed on tours. In consequence he played only two full seasons of county cricket; otherwise, apart from four overseas tours and ten home Tests, he spent his career as a professional in the leagues and minor counties. On the South African tour of 1913–14, he refused to appear in the fifth Test because the South African authorities had not provided the hotel accommodation he wanted for his wife. Since he had already taken forty-nine wickets in the preceding four Tests, there may have been some element of premeditation in their plan of hospitality. These were the two finest players—batsman and bowler—of their time. In their efforts to achieve what they believed to be a fair return for their labour they both behaved characteristically. Sydney Barnes employed the abrasive method, Jack Hobbs the quiet, diplomatic: and there can be little doubt that the second proved the more successful.

It is impossible to assess the effect of his shop on Jack Hobbs's cricket and his entire subsequent life, but certainly it was immense. Primarily it gave him the financial security which had been his aim since his childhood; eventually it went even beyond that; it proved so profitable as to provide him with a standard of genuine prosperity quite separate from his cricket. He continued to play professionally because he believed himself worthy of his hire, and because he had no wish for the standing of an amateur; he was proudly a professional but, at a pinch, an independent professional.

Another important influence in his life was religion. In accord with his upbringing, his faith was simple; his morality unquestioningly Christian. He went to church—Church of England—on most Sunday mornings and sometimes in the evenings; and often he went to revivalist meetings in the afternoon. Parsons of different denominations came to preach at his funeral. He was moved by evangelism; and, for a period of almost twenty years, he was a total abstainer on religious grounds. A man of high moral standards; he never bore grudges; rarely made even a gesture against what others might have thought an ill turn; and, in a game where competition has never been gentle, and where some tough ideas and words have always been exchanged, he never swore. At times it seemed that he was determined to show that he had deserved his success by his standard of morality. Relaxed, courteous, religious, modest; yet he had a jauntiness about him, a sense of fun, checkful mischief which kept him perpetually light in manner and behaviour.

Finally, one must consider his fitness. He had not the kind of childhood home where the most nourishing foods were regularly available. He built himself to a sound standard of height-weight-muscle ratio by exercise and reasonable eating. He was, all his life, a temperate man; he drank little at any time. The modestly fashionable soda-and-milk of the nineteen-twenties was a favourite of his; otherwise, in his playing days, he was generally content with milk, ginger beer or ginger ale. He preferred an evening at home to an evening out. On tour he might go to a music hall or to the cinema; but he would be early and quietly to bed. Batting was his fame, his excitement and his stimulus; family life his contentment.

He took steady exercise; generally in the form of golf, nets—bowling as well as batting—and conscientious fielding practice. He ate lightly and simply, homely English dishes; roast lamb or beef, green vegetables, fruit—especially apple pie—and cream or ice-cream. There can be no higher standard of fitness than that which enables a man of fifty-one to score a chanceless century against the County Champions.

He dressed quietly but fastidiously; dark grey suits; white shirts; a Surrey or England tie; well (self) polished shoes; his playing gear was always immaculate; such was his poise that it was virtually unknown for him to have a grass or mud stain on his flannels.

In a game which is decided by numbers, the prime

requisite is obviously the scoring of runs; the manner in which they are made, too, is important. Jack Hobbs was impressive in both directions. It is also revealing to understand his approach to cricket, and to batting in particular; and, although he could be the most determined attacker or resister, giving every ounce of concentration or determination to an innings, he always regarded it as a game and a pleasure. Greville Stevens who played against him many times recalled him with affectionate admiration—

Jack was a great man; not just a great batsman but a great man. In four consecutive Gentlemen-Players matches in 1925 and 1926, he only batted once in each of them and he scored 630 or so runs for three times out; I got him once and I suppose that cost me about a hundred and fifty runs, so I was economic. It was splendid to bowl at him; never easy, because whatever bad ball you bowled he would put away where there was no fieldsman. It became a thinking contest; almost like chess; he was working out what you would think, what you would do next; and he was so often right; you had barely let go of the ball than he was moving into position to hit it, because you had done what he thought you would do; and he would chuckle. Where he was so good was that, if you beat him—which didn't happen very often—he would chuckle too. Some batsmen cannot forgive themselves—or the bowler—or luck—for being out. Jack might be disappointed to be out, but he was never angry; he might sometimes shake his head if he had done something he thought was silly; but if a bowler had beaten him honestly, he would often admit it—not in a conceited way, modestly, but genuinely. He would say 'Well bowled' or salute you with his bat—and you felt as if you had been knighted.

This was the man—thus equipped—who in 1919, at the age of thirty-six stepped onto the fifteen-year high plateau of achievement in which he broke virtually all

the existing records for batting. The figures are so huge
that they can become meaningless: but, despite the gap
of a war and a season lost to injury and illness, he made
more runs and more centuries than anyone else in the
history of the game; set a new record for runs and
centuries scored in England-Australia Test matches;
shared in more century opening partnerships—166—
than anyone else; performed the unequalled feat of
scoring centuries in each innings of a match six times;
the highest aggregate—3024—in a season; sixteen
hundreds in a season (1925); the highest individual
score—316 not out for Surrey *v* Middlesex—ever made
at Lord's; seventeen seasonal aggregates of over 2,000
runs; most centuries—sixteen—in Gentlemen *v* Players;
the highest individual score—266—and shared the
largest opening stand—263, with Herbert Sutcliffe—
in those matches.

This made him, if not the first, one of the first British
sportsmen to be submitted to 'star treatment'. He was
less inclined to that than to batting. His shyness was
quite genuine; he was embarrassed by crowds calling
for him; distressed by barracking—even of another
player—and anxious to live a quiet life; batting, but
otherwise his own man. An invitation to appear on the
stage at the Coliseum alarmed him into precipitate
retreat; and all his life he protested that he was no
public speaker. It is true that he had a generally thin
voice which tended to crack under the nervous stress of
speech-making or broadcasting. He would, and did,
play—and play well and entertainingly—in many
charity matches; but he would not speak at cricket
dinners, solely because the idea of speaking filled him
with anxiety and something near revulsion. If his
opinion was asked in a meeting, he gave it quietly and
cogently but completely without elaboration; and,
although he was a humorous man, much addicted to

practical jokes, and enjoyed hearing a funny story, he was not a story-teller. He was, though, too good a batsman in a newly publicity-conscious age to escape the precocious but, as yet, relatively modest, media. He endorsed—not without payments for some, though not all—fountain pens, cricket bats and equipment, cocoa, total abstinence, chocolate and soft drinks. He was filmed, interviewed and provided with 'ghosts' who helped him to 'write' nine books, one of them a thriller called *The Test Match Surprise* which was something of a bestseller in the sixpenny 'Readers Library' so popular in Woolworths during the nineteen-twenties. The chief 'ghost' was the large and amiable Jack Ingham, who would not have claimed to be a great writer, but who was an extremely honest one. If he was ever tempted or pressed to go beyond the views or wishes of his 'body' he never did so; he was utterly faithful. As a result, we have in print Jack Hobbs's plain, unelaborate but revealing views on many matters, especially in the two later volumes of autobiography, *My Cricket Memories* (Heinemann, 1924) and *My Life Story* (*The Star*, 1935). After his playing days, too, he contributed his unspectacular, but eminently sound, views on Test matches through Jack Ingham to the now defunct London evening paper, *The Star*.

He believed firmly that a cricketer's concentration should never be broken by extraneous matters. He was once unusually brusque with an eminent portrait painter who stopped him and tried to make arrangements for a sitting on the stairs at Lord's as he was on his way out to bat in a Gentlemen *v* Players match.

He never cared to bat anywhere except first; he did not like to wait; and when he was not out after an interval, he liked to sit completely alone for a few minutes before he went out to bat. He was, though,

never tense and often did much to reduce tension in a
dressing room by a blend of humour and wisdom. It is
true that some of his contemporaries envied him; but
otherwise he had virtually no enemies. Most cricketers
are craftsmen and there were few who did not regard
him with respect, the majority with admiration; and
more than a few—most of them good enough batsmen
to appreciate his technique in depth and detail—with a
respect approaching awe. There was no malice in him;
much of his generosity was unmentioned; and few old
cricketers ever went to him for help without receiving
it.

All this prosperity, however, lay in the far from
certain future in 1919 when he embarked on the
amazing procession of record-breaking which would
have been accepted as incomparable but for his
splendid, if less arithmetically staggering, pre-War
virtuosity.

8

The Return

FOR English cricketers, 1919 was a summer of even greater euphoric relief than 1946 was for their sons. For some incomprehensible reason it was made a season of two-day matches; 11.30 am to 7.30 pm on the first day, 11.00 am to 7.30 pm on the second; often counties played three matches—Monday-Tuesday, Wednesday-Thursday and Friday-Saturday—a week; and the players soon became tired by—and of—such a programme.

Most of them, however, like Jack Hobbs, returned initially with an immense hunger for the game. In the Surrey trial match, against the bowling of Rushby, Peach, Hayes, Freeman and Harrison, he made a century in each innings; in the first he was out for 106 forty minutes before lunch; in the second he made 118, again in eighty minutes; he gave no chance in either innings. Then he galloped off with 64 and 86 at headlong rate against Somerset when *Wisden's* reporter noted, perceptively, 'Hobbs gave two brilliant displays, but in his cricket there was a suggestion of that over-eagerness which for a week or two in the first half of the season checked his progress.' The *Almanack's* final review noted:

Hobbs, just as much as in the seasons before the War, was the best bat in England. Early in the summer he had a brief spell of comparative failure, due to a little over-eagerness and over-confidence. He seemed to have an idea that, without waiting to get the pace of the ground, he could turn straight balls to square leg. However, he soon saw his error, and took more pains to play himself in.

It may be that this was for him the climacteric; that he had in fact lost the touch of his younger days. Yet it must be possible that he found the return to cricket so heady that, even by his pre-1915 standards, he over-reached himself. The extent of his self-discipline may be gathered from the fact that eventually he scored 2594 runs—707 more than anyone else—in the season. Talking of him at this time, Alec Kennedy, that monumentally steady medium pace bowler for Hampshire, once recalled:

There never was a better batsman than Jack Hobbs; and everyone who ever played with him knows that. It was not just that he was a text-book player; he was so much more than that. He was as brilliant as any Jessop or any player like that; and he was so certain with it. Once, just after the War, I started a match against him and the first ball I bowled was a late outswinger, it moved from about middle to off stump and he stepped across and hit it to square leg for four and—before I could say anything—he looked down the pitch and grinned and said 'I shouldn't have done that, should I?—I was a bit lucky.' That is how good he was; he was so sure of the ball; it was always hitting the middle of the bat. You used to feel he knew what you would do before you knew it yourself; and he was so certain when the ball was doing a bit off a 'green' pitch; it would move and you thought it was through; and there he was, waiting for it. He was the one batsman I never really thought I would beat and get out; I just used to keep on bowling and hope he would get himself out; he did that sometimes when he was tired or it all seemed too easy; but if he set out to stay in, you never had a chance; or at least I never did; and I don't know anyone else who did, or even thought he did.

In 1919, at The Oval, Hampshire put out Jack Hobbs for 15 and 38 and beat Surrey, which made a considerable difference to their eventual Championship position. In the first innings he lofted Kennedy's slower ball to Lionel Tennyson at mid-on. In the second he set out to change and win the match. He had made 38, was in touch and going well on the second morning, when Alec Kennedy slightly over-pitched to him. He stepped up and drove and that remarkable cricketer George Brown, four yards away at silly point, caught him, while everyone—the batsman included—looked for the ball on the cover boundary. Jack Hobbs said it was the finest catch he was ever out to: George Brown agreed enthusiastically, and added that a few minutes before he had been rubbing the previously bruised ball of his thumb with oil of wintergreen and that the ball hit his hand so hard that the maker's gold-leaf mark, entire, sharp and clear, peeled off on the film of wintergreen on his palm.

Then, for Jack Hobbs, the runs began to come plentifully. He scored—as no one else ever did—centuries in all three Gentlemen-Players matches; at The Oval, Lord's and Scarborough. Against the Australian Imperial Forces team, with Gregory, Kelleway, Lampard and Collins bowling, he carried his bat for 205 not out of a Surrey total of 344. In the first Kent match—at Blackheath where Surrey were so often beaten—he made a splendid 102 out of 203 (no one else made 30) against Woolley and Freeman on a turning wicket. The return, in August, was his long deferred benefit. He made only 17 in the first innings. When Kent were out for the second time, Surrey needed 95 to win in 43 minutes, and Donald Knight, acting captain of Surrey, sent Jack Hobbs and Jack Crawford in first in poor light and, soon afterwards, drizzle. Crawford hit from the start; Jack Hobbs played himself in for two overs and then also began to strike. One of the spectators there that day recalled, long afterwards, the striped awning running out above the pavilion windows and how a couple of straight sixes landing on them sent up splashes of rain. The 95 runs came in thirty-two minutes—Crawford 48, Hobbs, 47—and the batsmen were mobbed into the pavilion. When Jack Hobbs reached the dressing room, one of his batting gloves was missing but there was a one pound note in his bare hand. Batting with a damaged wrist for England against the Champion County—a mighty Yorkshire team—when two wickets fell early, he made a faultless 101.

This season saw the beginning of the third of the four great opening partnerships of Jack Hobbs's career, that with Andrew Sandham. Later, when the school holidays began, Donald Knight—at this time one of the best and most handsome batsmen in the country—was available, and Sandham had to stand down. Brought back in August and placed lower in the order, he established himself with a series of sound innings. Although, for a year or two, he sometimes dropped down the order to enable Donald Knight to go in with Hobbs, he remained a first choice for Surrey until his retirement in 1937.

Shorter than his partner—only five-feet-six—'Sandy' was a dapper, poised, unspectacular but outstandingly equipped batsman, unflinching against pace, quick of wit and movement in dealing with spin; an orthodox, wristy stylist, he was exceptionally strong off his legs, and a delicate cutter. Although he is numbered among the few cricketers who scored over a hundred centuries, and his 325 in West Indies in 1929–30 set a new record for an individual Test innings, he was, contentedly, the junior member of a partnership which made a hundred for the first wicket sixty-three times, a figure beaten only by Herbert Sutcliffe and Percy Holmes with sixty-nine.

In 1921, when injury and illness reduced Jack Hobbs's Championship appearances to a single match, Sandham assumed his responsibilities and finished with the highest aggregate and average for Surrey. Once described by Robertson-Glasgow as 'a first fiddle who for most of his time played second in the orchestra'; and a splendidly fast, safe outfield, in any other period he must surely have played in more than his fourteen Test matches.

Like Rhodes and Sutcliffe—and naturally a faster runner than either—Sandham ran well between the wickets with, and for, Jack Hobbs.

> I always watched him playing the ball, especially the last of an over and I was always backing up well down the wicket: no calling—if he started, we went. I remember being in with him once for a quarter-of-an-hour and only receiving one ball—and someone complained that I was being slow.

When he was the senior partner, Sandy could call the tune for himself; and Bob Wyatt still recalls, with a smile, that when the two batted together in the West Indies, in 1929–30, Sandham, by placing and quick starting, used constantly to take a single from the last ball or last-but-one of an over. A true Surrey man, born in Streatham, he played his early cricket there and with Mitcham and, from the time he joined the Surrey staff in 1910, he served the club as player, coach and scorer over the next sixty years.

Again in 1920, Jack Hobbs scored more runs than

anyone else in the country; this time the second man was 307 behind; and only three others were within 900 of him. Once more, too, in a season of no Test matches, he rose to high challenge with 215 for the Rest against the Champion County, on this occasion, Middlesex. He long cherished his innings against Leicestershire at Leicester that year. After Percy George Fender had looked at the pitch he said 'We don't want to bat more than once on this one!'—and performed the duty of a good captain by winning the toss and giving Surrey first innings. On a vicious, lifting wicket—three Leicestershire batsmen were so seriously injured in their first innings that they were unable to bat in the second—Jack Hobbs scored a century before lunch. On a late decision, hit-or-leave basis, he made 134 out of 177 for the first wicket with Andrew Sandham in little over an hour-and-a-half: he hit a six and nineteen fours and did not make a mistake; no one else on either side made fifty. Percy Fender, called to London on urgent business, handed over the captaincy to Hobbs and, when he returned on the second afternoon, Surrey had won by an innings and 105 runs. In the match with Kent, at The Oval, he scored 132 of an opening partnership of 196 with Andrew Sandham. To his amusement, largely because of his five for 21 against Warwickshire, he was top, not only of Surrey's, but also of the national, bowling averages, with 17 wickets at 11.82.

In the following winter, with Johnny Douglas's side which was butchered five-nil in Australia, he was first in the English Test batting with 50.5 (Douglas was next with 39.33). In a series marked by perfect batting conditions, he made a fine century on the one day of the one bad wicket in the entire rubber—a genuine Melbourne 'sticky'—when even survival was extremely difficult. He scored his 122 in three-and-a-half hours and did not give a chance until he had reached 110. His commanding century in the following Test—at Adelaide—was England's only serious gesture towards the 490 they needed to win. He scored 50 out of 66 for one overnight; 73 of his second wicket stand of 105 with Harry Makepeace; his final 123, out of 183, in two-and-a-half hours. The rest of the batting crumpled against one of the finest of all Australian attacks—McDonald, Gregory, Kelleway, Mailey, Armstrong and Ryder. In the second State match with New South Wales he severely damaged a thigh muscle but, although he was in considerable pain, John Douglas persuaded him to play in the fifth—Sydney—Test. Despite the handicap he made 40 and 34 but was hampered in the field and the injury was seriously aggravated.

This series saw the end of his opening partnerships with Wilfred Rhodes and in the third—Adelaide—Test, Rhodes was run out—only the second time that ever happened in their pairing, and the solitary occasion in Tests. Rhodes recalled, 'In all the time Jack and I batted together, I were only run out twice—and both times it were my fault.'

Percy Fender, in his astutely observed book on the series, *Defending the Ashes* (Chapman & Hall, 1921) wrote of this incident:

These two had made reputations for themselves in the past in connection with their short running and, as usual, they ragged the field right from the commencement. With the score at 25, however, in attempting what should have been quite an easy run, Rhodes made three mistakes. First, he did not start as soon as usual; secondly, he did not run straight, but swerved across the wicket as the ball was thrown, and left the fielder a clear shot at the wicket; and, thirdly, he did not run hard. McDonald, running from fairly close mid-on, threw the ball in underhand and hit the wicket. As Rhodes said afterwards, he could easily have been in but he made a mistake which was as inexplicable as it was unfortunate.

The two played in only one more Test team—that which achieved England's historic win at The Oval in 1926; but then they did not bat together. To the end of both their lives they held one another in considerable respect. Different as they were in temperament and character, they had in common immense integrity, high cricketing professionalism and outstanding skill. Their 323 at Melbourne in February 1912 is still the highest opening partnership in Anglo-Australian cricket.

There was a measure of puritanical Yorkshireness as well as immense, measured admiration in Wilfred's comment on Jack—'He could have scored thousands more runs but often he was content to throw his wicket away and give someone else a chance.' Wilfred did not use words like 'thousands' lightly.

It is, though, the measure of the man that his Test average is six runs an innings higher than his overall figure: and that he scored 700 more runs against Australia than any other Englishman.

9

Check and Accession

THE AUSTRALIANS and their beaten opponents
travelled on the same ship to the 1921 series in England,
and Jack Hobbs looked forward with interest—even
relish—to meeting their bowlers again. He did so in the
second—and unfamiliar—fixture of their tour, against
L. G. Robinson's XI at Attleborough, in Norfolk.
Lionel Robinson, a nephew of Edward Barton, the first
Prime Minister of Australia, was prominent in horse-
racing circles: he had a private ground on his estate at
Old Buckenham Hall; and he mustered a side including
ten English Test players. Unusually in that summer,
the game was played on a wet and difficult pitch on
which John Douglas and Clem Gibson bowled out the
Australians for 136. Then, against an attack of
Gregory, McDonald, Macartney, Mailey and Hendry,
Jack Hobbs proceeded to bat with such ease and
command that, looking back in after years, he was
inclined to rate it the best innings of his career.
Certainly Warwick Armstrong considered it as fine as
any played for or against the Australians on that tour.
He had made 85—substantially the highest individual
score of the match—when he went for a quick single.
His partner, Vallance Jupp, said that, as they crossed,
he heard the snap of his thigh muscle—the one
damaged at Sydney two months earlier. That proved
Jack Hobbs's last innings against the 1921 Australians.

By the end of June he was playing again and, effectively winning Surrey's match against Yorkshire, by carrying his bat through the innings for 172 not out in a total of 294, he made certain of his place for the third—Headingley—Test. On the first afternoon, however, he had to leave the field with acute stomach pains. The trouble was diagnosed as appendicitis, not then as well understood and simply treated as now. It was suggested that he should go back to London for treatment. Fortunately Mrs Hobbs decided the matter should be dealt with locally. Sir Berkeley Moynihan, who operated on him in a Leeds nursing home, told him later that he would not have survived a journey to London. He was grateful to be alive, but dragged down and weakened by the illness and the operation, he was unable to play any more cricket that summer. His final figures were six innings: 312 runs; 172 highest score; 2 not outs; 78.00 average.

He had still not shaken off the effects of the operation at the start of the 1922 season, and admitted to being less than fully fit. *Wisden* noted that 'Several times he seemed anxious to get out as soon as he had passed the hundred'. Nevertheless, he was second in the first-class averages with 2552 runs at 62.24.

At Scarborough for C. I. Thornton's XI against the MCC team for South Africa, he went in first with a young Yorkshireman, Herbert Sutcliffe, and unaware of what it presaged, they put on 120 for the first wicket. In the last match of the season, Champion County (Yorkshire) *v* The Rest of England, when the other ten 'Rest' batsmen made 99 between them, he scored exactly 100, his tenth century of the season which lifted his total to ninety-nine. Since he had decided not to go with MCC to South Africa in the intervening winter it was not until May 1923, in Surrey's second match—against Somerset at Bath—that he became the third batsman, following W. G. Grace and Tom Hayward, to reach a century of centuries, and Surrey presented him with a hundred guineas. Otherwise 1923 was the poorest season of his maturity. Still not fully fit, he made only three other centuries and was no more than third in aggregate and average (1595 at 41.97) for Surrey. At forty, some deterioration was to be expected. Not necessarily the end of his career, but some decline in eminence would seem probable. Certainly he could not have expected—nor realistically even have hoped—that he would make another ninety-seven centuries. Yet immediately he took out his quite phenomenal second lease of cricketing life. Second in the national averages of 1924, with 58.16 and six centuries, that year saw also the beginning of his greatest Test partnership, with Herbert Sutcliffe.

Sutcliffe was a batsman of immense application and thought; strong, fit, orthodox, determined. He had an immensely sound defence, drove powerfully through the off side; was arguably the best hooker of his age and could, at need, score quickly through a wide range of strokes. Above all, he was cool, beyond disturbance, the master of survival and the ultimate pragmatist of cricket. He, too, delighted to run quick singles and, in their entire joint career, only once, at the very end of their partnership, were they separated by a run out.

Meanwhile they had become the legendary opening pair of all cricket history. Sir Robert Menzies delighted to tell that he had only twice taken his wife to watch Test cricket, and each time she saw only two batsmen. On the first occasion, at Melbourne in 1925, Hobbs and Sutcliffe batted all day. The next time, at Lord's in 1926, when they arrived a few minutes after the start and as the English opening batsmen walked out Lady Menzies exclaimed 'Well I never, it's those two again'—and, when she and her husband had to leave, a few minutes before tea, they were still there.

In twenty-six of their partnerships—fifteen of them in Tests—they put up the hundred; in seven of them, over two hundred. Their entry into Test cricket was impressive. South Africa were the visiting side and, when their captain, Herbie Taylor, won the toss in the first Test at Edgbaston, he put England in to bat. Hobbs and Sutcliffe began with 136; England made 438. Then Maurice Tate and Arthur Gilligan bowled out South Africa for 30 and, although they batted well the second time, they lost by an innings. At Lord's where England batted second Hobbs (211) and Sutcliffe (122) put on 268 for the first wicket; at Leeds 72 and 17; and, after rain prevented them batting at Manchester, 5 at The Oval.

Their batting, and the bowling of Maurice Tate, formed England's main resistance to the Australian side that took the rubber of 1924–25 by four matches to one. Their opening partnerships were of 157 and 110; 283 and 36; 15 and 63; 126; 0 and 3. Maurice Tate, bowling with immense heart, zeal and life, set a new record with 38 wickets in an England-Australia series and, in the win—by an innings and 29 runs at Melbourne—the 'new' England side achieved its first major success against the old enemy. They were to confirm their quality at home in 1926.

First, though, perhaps surprisingly for one who believed that all-the year-round cricket made a player stale, Jack Hobbs came back to a most remarkable summer in 1925. At its beginning he had scored 113 centuries. In his first six matches for Surrey he made 34, 47, 104, 109, 120, 129 and 189: then, in successive innings in June, 107, 87, 104, 143 not out, 111 and 215 (in three-and-a-half hours out of a total of 376). With 140 in the Gentlemen *v* Players at Lord's and 105 against Kent at Blackheath, by the third week of July he had made a dozen centuries and was only one behind W. G. Grace's 126. What followed was virtually the first instance of what would now be called 'the pressure of the media' on cricket. Within a few years the record-breaking of Bradman and the Jardine-Larwood 'body-line' tactic were to make it common. For the moment it was new. W. G. Grace had been a considerable batsman-hero, but the press of his day was remote—it had never considered being anything else: news-film was unknown and wireless, television, the business of star-appeal, the personal 'quote', the interview and the whole concept of publicity lay in the future. Even in its 1925 form, however, it undoubtedly affected the batting of Jack Hobbs more profoundly than the bowlers of that season. A whole caravan of reporters, cameramen, photographers and feature writers fell in behind him; and the man who had made twelve centuries in sixteen matches now went six without seriously approaching such a figure. Even after a resistant 54—highest score but one for Surrey in the match—against the strong Nottinghamshire bowling in a crucial Championship match, an evening paper headline ran 'Hobbs Fails Again'. Even he, normally a placid man, began to find the whole affair fraying his nerves. The first day of Surrey's weekend match with Somerset drew large crowds hopeful of seeing the 'record' century made. In the event John Daniell won the toss and Somerset batted first. They were out though, before tea, leaving Surrey about two-and-a-quarter hours' batting. Almost as soon as he began Hobbs lofted a ball dangerously on the leg side; and, after Sandham was out early, and he was batting with D. J. Knight, he pushed to mid-on, called and ran as if he had been with Sandham. Knight had not started but, seeing Hobbs committed and stranded, he generously

—or sensibly—set out, crossed him, and was run out. Amateurs did not in those days often sacrifice their wickets for professionals, but these two were exceptional examples of both kinds. From that point onwards he set out calmly to resolve the issue by making a certain century. Somerset bowled tight; he was wise enough not to press for his hundred that night and was 91 not out at the close of play. Visiting cricket teams used, in those days, to stay at the hotel outside Taunton railway station; Jack left it on Sunday only to go to church and, as he sat over supper, he saw through the windows the press contingent streaming into town off the London train. He had kept the world waiting exactly four weeks for the hundred-and-twenty-sixth. Now John Daniell asked him if he would wait until all the crowd outside had been admitted before he started to bat. His courtesy extended even to that further strain, but once play began, he wasted no time. Three quickly pushed singles, a four off a no ball and he turned Jim Bridges to leg and equalled 'The Old Man's' record. Percy George Fender brought out a wine glass assumed to contain champagne or whisky and soda—in fact it was ginger ale—the entire fielding side shook his hand, cameras clicked, the crowd cheered: one run later he was caught off Bridges and, at last, after four weeks, the publicity posse left him and went back to London. So, when Somerset, recovering in their second innings, left Surrey 183 to win, he went out at his ease, struck the first ball through the covers for four and proceeded, in an innings at once carefree, elegant and chanceless, to score the century by which he actually exceeded Grace's record. Sandham, with his invariable consideration, did not hurry, but left him the space to reach his second century of the match with the winning hit in an almost empty ground.

Among the few spectators was Morley Richards,

later to become a nationally known journalist, but then a young reporter on the local paper. He had recently married but had not been able to afford a honeymoon. Now, as the only newspaperman on the ground, he sold the story of the century which beat W. G. to virtually every paper in the country—and took his wife to Torquay for a fortnight on the proceeds. Thirty-six years afterwards, over a luncheon of The Master's Club, he took that first opportunity to tell the Master the story and thank him for that unexpected honeymoon. Jack Hobbs's reaction was typical 'Really? well I never, well I *am* glad—yes, I am—I wish I had known that then—thank you for telling me.' With two more hundreds—one of them a perfect 106 made in two-and-a-half hours against the Champion County, Yorkshire —he set a new record of sixteen in a season. He was, too, top of the averages with an aggregate (3024) nearly six hundred more, and an average over ten better, than anyone else in the country.

Surrey opened a subscription list for him and offered him a benefit in 1926; Cambridge gave him a civic dinner and the local council asked if they might name the new pavilion on Parker's Piece after him. He was delighted; he always cherished a deep affection for Cambridge and for Parker's Piece—his cricket 'school' —in particular. He went happily, if shyly, to perform the opening ceremony. Unhappily, in later years, the pavilion, in use generally as a tea room, fell on poor days. In 1978 a local restaurant owner bought it to convert it into a bistro; and was reported in *The Cambridge Evening News* to have applied to the council for permission to change its name. A letter to that paper evoked some local protest and, eventually, a letter from the City Secretary to say 'The Hobbs Pavilion will retain its title'.

Less than a year later it was taken over by Stephen

and Tessa Hill who were concerned from the outset to emphasise the Hobbs connection. Their aim was to create an establishment in tune with modern town and University; yet as relaxed as the Parker's Piece setting indicated. In a bistro-style restaurant, they offered croissants, cakes and coffee in the morning; licensed, they served both wines and beer with their home-made soups, paté, salads, casseroles and cheesecake at lunch; in the afternoon, cream teas; and, in the evening, supper with appropriate wines. Such a happy arrangement deserved success. It is in *The Good Food Guide*.

Jack was not ill-pleased, either, at the payments he was offered for his endorsement of various commodities. He was, however, slightly alarmed by the invitation to play the lead—with a suitable leading lady—in a film; and by Sir Oswald Stoll's offer of £250 a week to appear in a cricket 'Scena' at the Coliseum; he backed hastily away from both.

Surrey were runners-up in the Championship. Between the two wars their bowling—despite Fender's shrewd handling and versatility—was never quite equal to that of Yorkshire, nor of Lancashire, in their best years.

Season now followed season in almost processional success. If he had thought 1925 his finest summer, 1926 was to give him in many ways even greater satisfaction. He was disappointed at Surrey's fall from second to fifth position, their lowest in the eight seasons since the war; they had only been once lower (seventh in 1912) and only twice as low in the table in his pre-war years. In fact they did not improve on fifth place for the rest of his years in the side. The Oval wickets were too much for their bowling, which was always one—often two—men short of top class.

For the rest, it was a year for celebration. It can be said that no match result in his career gave him deeper pleasure than the win in the fifth Test at The Oval to take back The Ashes. That game, too, saw the high moment of the now legendary Hobbs-Sutcliffe partnership. Although several other major batsmen played over a dozen innings more than his forty-one, his aggregate was 100—and his average 11—runs higher than any other player in the country. He averaged 81 in the Test series against Australia, with two centuries, one of them in the decisive Oval match which gave England the rubber and The Ashes. He and Wilfred Rhodes were co-opted as members of the selection committee —the first professionals ever invited into those councils: and, when Arthur Carr fell ill at Leeds, he was given charge of the England team in the field. Of his ten centuries, his 316 not out against Middlesex was—and remains—the Lord's record; and he derived much satisfaction from a defensively sound 102 against a Yorkshire side on the kill.

After the four previous Tests with Australia were drawn, that at the Oval was to be the first in England to be played to a finish. The Trent Bridge game was reduced by rain to less than an hour's play in which Hobbs and Sutcliffe made 32. Jack Hobbs's 119 at Lord's; 49 and 88 at Headingley; 74 at Old Trafford and 100 at The Oval were all the highest-but-one scores of the respective England innings. In the event, the fifth match was settled in four days, but the simple fact that it could be played to a finish undoubtedly influenced the tactical thinking of both sides.

Some few incidents of the first day of that match survive sharply in the memory of the schoolboy for whom it was not only a first sight of Jack Hobbs or a Test match, but a first sight of first-class cricket. Public interest was immense and intense; newspaper forecasts of huge crowds and the gates being closed early daunted many; but enabled some to get reasonable seats in a relatively small and extremely good-natured crowd.

The young Chapman had taken over from Carr as captain of England. In truth he leant heavily—and rightly—on the advice of Hobbs and Rhodes, whose tactical acumen was ruefully admitted and admired by Australians. Chapman won the toss and England batted. To one seeing him for the first time, the remarkable aspect of Jack Hobbs's batting was that it looked so calmly matter of fact that only Sutcliffe's portentous care at the other end suggested that batting was other than simple. He strolled, pushed, deflected, once or twice drove Mailey, swept Grimmett. It all seemed so inevitable when his old friend and enemy, Arthur Mailey, bowled him a high full toss. Hobbs identified the gap wide of mid-on and went casually to hit a four through it when the ball hung or dipped—who knows, the batsman did not—and hit the stumps. Most memorably, after looking for a moment completely flabbergasted, Jack threw back his head and laughed. Perhaps he was wrong. Imagine a Boycott, a Chappell, a Turner or a Gavaskar, laughing when he was bowled by a slow full toss. Perhaps Jack Hobbs was wrong to regard cricket as a matter for mirth. Yet, in that same summer, he had set a new record for an individual total of runs in Tests between England and Australia. He and Mailey exchanged a few cheerful words as he set off for the pavilion.

England made 280; Australia led by 22 on the first innings and Hobbs and Sutcliffe made 49 in an hour to the close of play on Monday. On Monday night a spectacular thunderstorm broke over south London, drenching the uncovered Oval wicket. Play began on time, at eleven, and, after the first over, bowled by Grimmett, the two batsmen, as shrewd assessors of a pitch as any, met in midwicket with 'The rain has done us'—'Yes, I'm afraid so'. Even 'Sailor' Young, the umpire, chimed in with 'Yes, bad luck, that's right'. On such a pessimistic note began one of the legendary partnerships of Test cricket which was to instal Hobbs and Sutcliffe in the history—and the mythology—of cricket as the greatest of all opening pairs.

Apart from his fast-bowler, Jack Gregory, the Australian captain, Herbie Collins, could use Arthur Richardson, a slow to medium off-spinner; Charlie Macartney, slow left-arm; and Arthur Mailey, the leg-spinner, an artful tactician but not so accurate as English captains expect their spin bowlers to be on a sticky wicket. Macartney and Richardson, the two orthodox finger spinners, were the types an experienced English captain would have used in these circumstances. An Australian 'sticky' is, of course, different in character to the English; it is usual there to employ medium pace bowlers who derive disconcerting lift from a drying pitch. For this reason, finger spinners from overseas rarely develop the peculiar skills of the English, notably the ability to bowl round the wicket when the ball is turning. Macartney, who had concentrated much on his batting since the war, began the bowling with Grimmett; but Collins soon replaced him with Richardson whom he gave a closely set leg-side field. Arthur Richardson began by bowling over the wicket when the ball 'did' so much that, if it pitched outside the stumps, the batsman could play it with his pads but, when it pitched 'on', it turned so much that it missed the leg stump. Jack Hobbs lifted his first ball over the short legs for four. It was obvious, though, that as the wicket dried the off-spinner would prove difficult by his turn and unpredictable lift. Like many otherwise talented off-break bowlers from overseas—Lance Gibbs and Athol Rowan are notable examples—he simply had no experience of bowling round the wicket; and that is not a knack to be assimilated quickly. Similarly, at Old Trafford in 1956, when Jim Laker took nineteen Australian wickets, their off-spinner—Ian Johnson who, as captain, could put himself on at any time or end he wanted—was completely innocuous.

Eventually, after Hobbs had several times swept the ball which spun across him, Collins set a six-man leg trap and directed Richardson to bowl round the wicket. When the pitch was at its worst, he bowled ten overs—eight of them to Jack Hobbs—for two runs; the crowd, tautly silent, conscious of the crisis. Both Hobbs and Sutcliffe were vastly experienced in playing off spin on turning pitches, but in such conditions Richardson ought to have broken the English batting. Hobbs employed effectively the tactical gambit of taking guard a foot outside his leg stump and moving across to play the ball, which clearly disconcerted Richardson. At the other end, Mailey, whom he greeted with 'No full tosses this time, Arthur'—was not dangerous. By containing Richardson with such deep defensive respect, Hobbs clearly kept off Macartney who might have been Australia's sharpest edge in such conditions. However that may be, Sutcliffe adhered; Hobbs took every chance to attack; the two opening batsmen were still in at lunch when the score was 161 for no wicket (Hobbs 97, Sutcliffe 53); and, equally important, the wicket was beginning to ease.

M. A. Noble has suggested that Hobbs deliberately made Richardson look difficult so that Collins would keep him on rather than using Macartney from his end, which was the more difficult of the two. Jack Hobbs always studiously refrained from commenting on that. He did, though, once say:

Of course Richardson was difficult to play—any finger spinner would be on a wicket like that—and the ball popped so much and so often that either of us could easily have been out. But, of course, he was not used to bowling on that kind of pitch—I don't think we could have stayed as long as we did against Cec Parkin or Ewart Astill or George Macaulay either.

He reached his century with a tiny dab off Gregory which travelled barely a yard towards point but he and Sutcliffe were safely home for a typical quick single. His century was chanceless and, despite the difficulties of the conditions, took only three-and-a-half hours. The crowd stood and cheered him in a fashion which moved him in recollection all his life; and he, extravagantly, by his standards, waved both his cap and his bat. A moment later Gregory flicked away his off bail; but the peril of defeat had been averted; and advantage established. Even Jack Hobbs never played a more valuable innings. Sutcliffe batted through to the end of the day when he was bowled by Mailey for 161.

Between them Hobbs and Sutcliffe scored 261 of England's 436 and, until Maurice Tate came in at number nine and threw his bat, no one else made more than 27. The nature of the pitch is indicated, too, by the fact that so good a wicket-keeper as Oldfield allowed 37 extras. It grew little better; Australia never looked like scoring the 415 they needed to win against Larwood and Rhodes, the youngest and the oldest of the English bowlers, and England took the match by 289 runs, the rubber and The Ashes.

It is said that, before Oxford University's match at The Oval in 1926, one of their officials hinted to the Surrey authorities that they considered it a slight that so many of the county's better players were rested for that fixture. When the University were out for 273, Hobbs and Sandham made 44 together overnight; next day they batted on to 276 before a storm stopped play. On Friday, although the pitch played awkwardly, they took their partnership to 428 (made in only a little over four hours) then second only to the 554 of Brown and Tunnicliffe for the first wicket in English cricket, before Sandham was out. Jack Hobbs batted on until after lunch for 261.

Next morning he appeared at Lord's for the second Test with Australia and, when someone asked if he did not feel tired, he said he did not—only a little stiff. He may have been happy that he had not to open the innings that morning; but when he did, on Monday, he and Sutcliffe put on 182; and he himself scored 119.

After two such years, 1927 was a disappointment. In Surrey's first Championship match—against Hampshire—Jack scored a century in each innings; but he missed a dozen matches through a skin infection and a leg injury. Nevertheless, he scored a century at a run a minute before lunch against Nottinghamshire in the Bank Holiday match. His average of 52 would have been enough for most men.

A torn thigh muscle in 1928 cost him six weeks' cricket, including the first of the three Tests with West Indies; but he scored 53 in the second and 159 in the third. For the Rest against the Champion County—Lancashire—he made 150 in two-and-a-quarter hours; and he averaged 82.

Normally a mild-tempered man, he felt unjustly treated when he was left out of the Lord's Gentlemen-Players match without being asked whether he was fit. He devoted much attention to—and derived immense pleasure—from scoring a century against Kent in the match before that fixture.

In that same season, still only semi-fit, he captained an all-professional Surrey team which bowled out Northamptonshire for 302 with about an hour left for play before the end of the first day. Andrew Sandham was away ill and, looking down the team list, he saw good reasons why several of the players should not go in first. When Ted Brooks, the wicket-keeper (normally number ten) suggested he should go in with him, he replied, in a characteristic joke,

> 'No Ted, I don't think you're a good enough batsman—I shall take Alfred.'

So Alf Gover—normally number eleven—to his remembered pride, went in first with The Master. In that position of eminence, though, he experienced considerable trouble in playing Austin Matthews, lively fast-medium, who was later to open the bowling for England. At the end of the over Jack walked down the wicket—

> 'You don't fancy Austin, Alf, do you?'
> 'No,—I don't.'
> 'What about Stretton?' (the other opening bowler)
> 'Oh, I think I can deal with him.'
> 'All right then, I'll take Austin.'

So he proceeded to 'farm' Matthews, playing him quite comfortably. He was leaning into an in-swinger to push it on the leg side when it moved the other way off the seam. As Matthews half raised an arm, believing he was through, Hobbs, with extremely rapid adjustment but no impression of haste, rocked back and cut it wide of cover point's left hand for four. Austin Matthews twisted round in his follow-through and said to Dick Burrows, the umpire—

> 'What bloody chance have I got?'
> 'None at all, mate,' said Burrows, himself a former bowler who in his time had suffered at those same hands, 'None at all if the old man feels like that.'

Amusedly he ensured that Matthews never had another ball at Gover that night: and they went in 49 for no wicket. Next morning Matthews bowled Gover in his first over; Jack Hobbs went on to a splendid century, and Surrey won by ten wickets.

At forty-five he still found batting a pleasure; and he enjoyed the company of cricketers. He had a great reputation as a practical joker; for years he delighted in saying to a friend about to leave him—'Is this your pen? and is this your lighter? this your cigarette case? this your handkerchief?'—all adroitly removed from his pockets while his attention was directed elsewhere. He delighted, too, in scaring the next man in. Once, in a Gentlemen-Players match at The Oval, he laid on all for 'Lofty' Herman, of Hampshire, who was absorbed in writing a letter. Jack Hobbs organised a few of the players into a concerted 'He's out', 'Lofty' hastily put down his pen, picked up bat and gloves and, with Patsy Hendren acting as a decoy, diverting his attention from the play by trotting at his side warning him about the bowlers, he was actually about halfway down the pavilion steps before he realised what had been done to him.

In Test matches at Lord's, free drinks were provided at lunch though not for tea, which was served in the dressing-room. Percy Chapman used habitually to order an extra couple of large gin-and-tonics and pour them into a ginger beer bottle which, without realising that anyone noticed it, he used to hide in his bag to drink in the tea interval. One hot afternoon he came in from the field, went to his bag, opened the bottle and, with a beatific expression, tilted back his head and drank. His face changed—someone had substituted water for gin and tonic. In a second he knew who it was 'It's that bloody Jack Hobbs' he said as everyone in the dressing-room—all warned of the trick—erupted in laughter.

Fred Boyington, the Surrey scorer before the First World War, was extremely fussy about his clothes—and also fairly close with money. No one could understand why he endured Jack Hobbs snatching his hat and kicking it about the room or the street. It was years before they discovered that, two or three times a season, Jack used to buy him a new hat for that privilege.

Jack Hobbs made a living—by the standard of most of his contemporaries a most handsome one—by playing the game of cricket; and, to the end, he found it fun.

10

The Last Round

BY NOW even the latest event was nostalgic. The tour
of 1928–29 was his fifth—and Mrs Hobbs's second—to
Australia and on one of the great grounds after another
the crowds bade him an affectionate and admiring
farewell. He was no longer the major English batsman;
on figures that was Walter Hammond, maturing to the
achievement which matched his ability. Still Jack
Hobbs averaged 50 for the Test series. He and Sutcliffe
mustered 85 for the first wicket at Brisbane; 105 at
Melbourne (third Test); 143 at Adelaide; 64 in the fifth
at Melbourne, when his 142 was the highest score of the
match. At the age of forty-six he became the oldest
player ever to score a century in an England-Australia
Test. In the earlier, Melbourne, Test rain made the pitch
spiteful when England needed 332 to win the match
and take the rubber. Jack himself did not think they
had a chance of doing it in those conditions. Once
more, however, he and Sutcliffe exhibited their pecu-
liarly English talent for batting calmly and soundly on a
bad wicket. After they had survived for an hour, he
thought there might be an outside chance if the innings
could be sustained until the conditions improved. He
signalled for a new bat and when the twelfth man
brought out a choice he went through the motions of
testing them, kept the one he was already using, but
sent back to Percy Chapman the message that, if a

wicket fell, Douglas Jardine—rather than Hammond, Chapman or Hendren, who were before him in the first innings—should be sent in. Eventually, at 105, when Hobbs was lbw to the off-spinner, Don Blackie, Jardine took his place and batted with typical care into the next day for 33, when he was out, at 199 for two, on a better pitch. Still five more wickets fell, but Sutcliffe's devoted and resourceful 135 saw England home.

Back home alternating ill fortune and consistent brilliance marked his summer of 1929. An illness in May and, later, a shoulder injury—incurred when he fell jumping for a catch at cover in the Test trial—cost him six weeks' play and hampered him in other matches; and he missed the first four of the Tests against South Africa. He scored a mellow 52 in an hour-and-a-quarter in the last; and was top of the first-class averages with an average of 66.55 (ten centuries). His batting was not merely the accumulation of runs; it was still a virtuoso performance.

He was desperately keen to do well in 1930. He knew his great period had already lasted beyond all reasonable limit but he wanted to go on playing as long as he could play well. He made a magnificent start to the season with 137 and 111 not out—and only one half chance in the two innings—against Glamorgan; then, in succession for Surrey, 66; 73, 57; 21; 27, 15; 34, 75; 83, 17.

Once more he was co-opted to the Selection Committee: and there he several times argued that he should stand down in favour of a younger man. Reasonably enough in view of his form, he was over-ruled; and in the first Test at Trent Bridge he fully justified his place with 78 and 74—top scores of both English innings—and decisive in their narrow win by 93 runs. This, however, was Bradman's series; he scored 974 runs at an average of 139.14 and Australia took the rubber by two to one. Hobbs averaged no more than 33.44 (but Hammond's figure was only 34). At Leeds, he was run out when Sutcliffe called for a run for a stroke to deep mid-off where Bradman, at high speed, picked up, shrewdly threw to the distant end, and hit the stumps to which Hobbs was running.

In the second innings of the final Test—his last appearance against Australia—he might perhaps have been saved until the next morning rather than sent in for the last hour after a day in the field. He had, though, never asked to be protected, and he did not now. As he walked to the wicket, the Australian team lined up, and Woodfull called for three cheers for Jack Hobbs: it was a profoundly moving occasion. He seemed in no trouble, played some smooth strokes, and had made nine out of 17 with Sutcliffe when he aimed to play a short ball from Fairfax to third man, it moved in, he under-edged it on to the ground and it bounced up on to the stumps.

He announced his retirement from Test cricket with gratitude for past success, and no bitterness. *Wisden* noted that, in five seasons from 1926 to 1930 he had, through representative games, illness and injury, missed fifty-three out of Surrey's 136 Championship fixtures. In that season, though, he passed W. G. Grace's record career aggregate of runs: scored five centuries, and averaged 51.29.

Still the runs came; and even the hardest-headed of professional cricketers were amazed at the relaxed ease of his batting. In 1931 he scored 2,418 runs at 56.23 with ten centuries. At Scarborough he and Sutcliffe put on 243 in 190 minutes for Players *v* Gentlemen; and his 153 off the New Zealanders was described by their captain, Tom Lowry, as the best innings played against that touring side. At a time when Sutcliffe, Hammond, Duleepsinhji, Woolley, Paynter and Jardine were playing, that was a considerable compliment to a man of forty-eight.

In 1932, despite a torn leg muscle, he scored 1,764 runs and averaged 56.90, and Douglas Jardine called his 161 not out at Lord's in his last Gentlemen-Players match 'a great personal triumph'. With it he broke W. G.'s record of fifteen centuries in those fixtures; and he set a fresh one—against Essex of sorry memory—by making two centuries in a match for the sixth time. There seemed to be no end to it all. In the winter of 1932–33 he went to Australia—taking Mrs Hobbs with him—to report the Test series there. On his return he found the spring chilly and did not begin his season until late May when, in his first innings, he scored 211 against West Indies at the Oval. He played only eighteen innings in the season yet he scored six centuries and was third in the first-class averages with 1,105 runs at 61.38.

He was by no means certain that he ought to try to play county cricket in 1934. He was in part persuaded to do so by a letter from George Duckworth reminding him of his promise made years before, to play in his— George's—benefit. Although it fell in such an un- promising part of the season as late May, he had chosen the Lancashire-Surrey fixture as his match. The draw- ing power of Jack Hobbs in those years ensured that he honoured his promises. In the event he again played only eighteen innings but this time at an average of 36.70 to end his first-class career. Yet even this last season, when he was rising fifty-two, was not without distinction.

He made 50 against MCC 'in his own masterly style' according to *Wisden* and then played in the first Championship match when Glamorgan made 352 on a good, first day wicket and John Clay twice bowled out Surrey on a 'turner'. No other Surrey batsman made more than 21 but Jack Hobbs, batting, John Clay recalled, made 17 and 'as if he was showing the boys how' a quite memorable and chanceless 62.

He had a couple of indifferent games, before he went up to Old Trafford for George Duckworth's benefit match. Lancashire were County Champions that year; only one century was scored against them at Old Trafford, and it was made by Jack Hobbs. He and Sandham put on 184 for the first wicket and he went on to 116, which took him four hours; and gave Surrey a first innings lead. In the second innings he made 51 not out. He was cheered all the way to the wicket and when he came in after his century, the crowd stood and sang Auld Lang Syne which almost proved too much for him.

For a man of fifty-one-and-a-half it was a remarkable feat of stamina alone. Questioned about it years afterwards he said—

'Oh, it was a terrible innings.'

'But George Duckworth says you never made a mistake.'

'Well, I don't think I gave a chance if that's what he means, but, you see, my timing was all wrong: I had really reached a stage where I didn't fancy running anyone's runs—not even my own—and towards the end I was just standing still and pulling everything through mid-on for four.'

The bowlers he was 'pulling through mid-on for four' were Frank Sibbles, Frank Booth, Len Hopwood, Jack Iddon and Frank Watson.

In June, on a lively bowler's wicket at Horsham he played an innings of highly skilful defence against the currently strong Sussex side. He made 79—the next Surrey score was 23—and seemed well on his way to a century when, to his enduring annoyance, he ran himself out.

He rested from a few matches but came back—and batted at number four—in the home game against Somerset at the Oval. That was his last county game at the Oval; not because he made only 15 but because some spectators barracked him—of all people—for misfielding a ball at cover. It hurt him the more because it happened at—of all places—'his' Oval.

He resolved not to play again; but the Glamorgan Club, feeling, with good reason, that his presence would improve the gate and their precarious exchequer—pressed him to play against them at Cardiff in the last match of the season. He was out of practice—he had not played since June—but he allowed himself to be persuaded; and in his only innings was lbw to John Clay for 0. It was an oddly unsatisfactory way to end so great a county career. Perhaps he might have stage-managed a better exit: but then, he was never a stage-manager.

So he went off, with Mrs Hobbs, to the Folkestone Festival where he etched a vignette innings of 38 against the Australians: and made 24 and 18 in a Gentlemen-Players match and, without realising it, walked out of first-class cricket for ever.

That summer the Hobbs Gates at the Oval were officially opened; an intelligently graceful compliment to pay a man during his lifetime rather than posthumously. That winter he sent the Surrey committee his courteous but unequivocal decision to retire. They, in return, made him an honorary life member of the Club.

From time to time he played for a Surrey Club and Ground or in a charity match, and the headmaster of Kimbolton School, an old friend, used regularly to ask him down there to play against the boys. When he went there in 1941 he was fifty-eight: he scored a century and walked off not knowing that it was his last; and went home, put up his bat, pad and boots, not knowing it was for ever.

11

The Old Master

ESSENTIALLY a man of his period, Jack Hobbs would never have made a pop-age star. He was an idol to at least two generations of cricket followers all over the world; and because he was as modest, honest and kind as he seemed, he virtually had not an enemy. His shop in Fleet Street became a place of pilgrimage for people from all the cricketing countries. Until the end of his days he received a huge mail, from every kind of request, to congratulations and friendly correspondence. He did not find writing easy, and his script was rather cramped; nevertheless, he insisted on answering every one of those letters in his own hand. All offers to have them duplicated—for a birthday or such occasion —or typed, were firmly refused. If people were 'kind enough' to write to him, he would write back to them; and, after his birthday, he would set aside often as much as a couple of hours a day, for two or three weeks, to clear the backlog.

When his playing days were over, his two interests were his family—always the first priority in his mind— and his business. His three sons and his daughter were all given faithful starts in life; and he was too wise to press the boys into cricket once he realised they had no outstanding aptitude for the game: but he saw them all settled into jobs as fitting and secure as possible.

When they were grown up and had left home, he

settled happily into a flat in Hove with his wife. Until a few months before he died, he went regularly into the shop on Mondays, Wednesdays and Fridays, meticulously keeping the books, settling accounts and meeting callers of all degrees of importance.

Sometimes he would issue his favourite summons, ringing up to say—

'Good morning; what a nice day.'
'Good morning, yes—how are you?'
'I'm well, and you?'
'Very well, thank you.'
'Couldn't you feel a bit better?'
'Well . . .'
'Good, come on over then; see you in the cellar.'

That meant the cellar of the Wellington Restaurant next door, an establishment kept by an amiable Belgian, Emil Haon, who was devoted to Jack and who used to sell him champagne, and sometimes share it with him. It would have affronted Jack's slightly puritan conscience to drink a bottle—or even a half-bottle—of champagne by himself; but he enjoyed sharing one. A bottle between three was his ideal prescription. It made a bad morning seem fine—and a fine one finer—he used to say.

One day in 1953 by a series of happy coincidences, the ration became two bottles between four—and Emil. Afterwards the four of us went up to the restaurant above where Emil served a splendid meal and, quite fortuitously, that was the first and founding meeting of 'The Master's Club'. Its only rules were that Sir Jack Hobbs was its perpetual guest of honour; that there was no subscription; no officers; no speeches and that the only toast was of 'The Master'. The members were a cross-section of his friends and admirers—Alf Gover, Frank Lee, John Marshall,

Kenneth Adam, Tom Pearce, John Bridges, Doug Insole, Greville Stevens, Harold Redding, Bev Lyon, Alec Durie, Hugh Metcalfe, Colin Cowdrey, Morley Richards (who reported the hundred-and-twenty-seventh century), the Bedser twins, Arthur Gilligan, Tom Wisdom, Bernard Hollowood, and myself.

The fixed occasion of the year has always been lunch on 'The Master's' birthday—16th December—or, when it fell at the weekend, on the Friday before or Monday afterwards. Other lunches happened spontaneously, even haphazardly; though over a period they were held on the Wednesday before a Lord's or Oval Test, when the visiting Test captain was usually a guest.

Menus, of course, have varied but the Birthday lunch has generally been Sir Jack's favourite meal, soup, roast beef and baked potatoes, apple pie and cream, cheese and celery: a dry white wine as an apéritif, burgundy with the beef and port with the cheese.

Until 1957, when The Wellington closed after the death of Emil, the lunches were always held there; then for a year at The Mitre; from 1958 generally at The Bedford Head (later called Henri's) until 1966 when a move was made to St Stephen's Tavern near the Houses of Parliament. Then, in 1978, at the suggestion and invitation of Raman Subba Row, to the Surrey Committee Room at The Oval. Such a headquarters with its opportunity of permanence gave the Club the promise of continuity.

Members could bring their own guests to ordinary lunches—which, in fact, were very rarely ordinary—but on the main occasion of the year—The Master's Birthday—the club acted as host to men who had played for England with him. The names read like a roll of honour of thirty years of English cricket—Herbert Sutcliffe, George Gunn, Maurice Tate, 'Plum' Warner,

'Tich' Freeman, Jack Crawford, George Brown, Patsy Hendren, George Geary, Ian Peebles, Bert Strudwick, Arthur Wellard, Bob Wyatt, Bill Hitch, Frank Woolley, George Duckworth, Leslie Ames, Walter Robins. There, too, for good measure were Andrew Sandham —now the guest of honour, who has proposed the toast of 'The Master' every year since Sir Jack's death— Learie Constantine, Sir Norman Birkett, Arthur Mailey, Don Bradman, Frank Tyson, Jack Mercer, Tom Webster, Jack's two sons, Jack and Len, 'Father' Marriott, Ted Dexter.

The 'no speeches' rule deferred to 'The Master's' life-long dislike of speech-making. On one birthday, however, to everyone's amazement, he stood up after the toast and with 'This isn't a speech, only a thank you' he went round the table mentioning everyone present by name with something light, often amusing, but never malicious, about each of them. It was, he said, the first speech he had ever made of his own free will; and he continued to do so every year until the last. He was the most gracious and popular of guests and one day confided that the idea at first alarmed him but now he was extremely proud of 'this club you friends made for me'.

He was knighted in 1953, but long before that he had won the accolade of public respect and affection. He needed to make no change in his life to be in order to bear the title as to the manner born. There is no doubt, though, that when he received the intimation of the honour to be bestowed—'I am asked by the Prime Minister to inform you . . .' he was genuinely surprised, even flustered. After some thought he did something he had never done before, and sought an interview with Sir Walter Monckton, then both President and Chairman of the Surrey Cricket Club. Unmistakably anxious, he asked Sir Walter most pressingly to use his influence to stop what he called 'all this' which, he felt was extravagant, embarrassing, even worrying. Monckton, a wise man, concealed his amusement, and pointed out almost sternly that this was not an honour bestowed simply on Sir Jack, but on all cricket—and on English professional cricketers. He had no reply to that; he accepted with an almost naïve mixture of pride, dignity and shyness; and spent several subsequent weeks embarrassedly adjuring his friends not to call him 'Sir'.

As Lady Hobbs became increasingly frail and ill, her husband nursed her both tenderly and skilfully. He would have someone in to sit with her during the days when he went up to London—when he would be back by four o'clock. For the rest, he took complete care of her. He would not have a resident nurse because that, he said, would destroy the intimacy of their relationship. For the last few years of her life he bathed, dressed, undressed and nursed her: combed her hair and adjusted her hat to her liking: cooked and cleaned for her. He certainly feared that, if he were to die, she would be put in a home; and he could not bear that thought. In March 1963, Lady Hobbs—his Ada—died. He had discharged his duty. He did not wish himself dead; he relaxed. A lump in his chest was diagnosed as cancer. Still through that summer he liked to take a morning glass of champagne with a friend and muse, not only about the past, but also the present. He liked to see Dexter batting and often he would go quietly down to the county ground at Hove and sit unrecognised, at the end near the gate, and watch him for an hour or two; then back to his flat. Through the autumn he grew a little thinner, a little more wan. His last excursion was to be a godfather at a christening in Hampshire. There came the day when to his poignant surprise he found he could no longer enjoy his champagne, though he firmly insisted that his friends should 'drink it for me'. There was no pain, he simply and uncomplainingly slipped away. His daughter Vera, who looked after him, said rightly 'He recognises you with his eyes'; and only a few hours before the end, he stroked the hand of his small godson with infinite gentleness. He lived through his eighty-first birthday and, on 21 December 1963, he died in his sleep.

This was the man who, without believing it to be a matter of major importance, made more runs than anyone else. There are the record books to prove that; and some photographs and film strip to show the splendid mastery of his batting method. Those who played with and against him generally considered him—in all conditions, on all pitches and against all types of bowling—the finest batsman. In the memory of those who knew him he was, too, a modest, gentle, kindly man with a streak of flawless steel which he revealed only when honour demanded it.

Statistics

John Berry Hobbs; born Cambridge, 16 December 1882; died Hove, 21 December 1963. Knight, cr. 1953; honorary life member Surrey C.C.C. 1934; honorary member M.C.C. 1949. Played Cambridgeshire 1904; Surrey 1905–1934; England 1907–1930. In first-class cricket, 1905–1934, scored 61,237 runs and 197 centuries. They were made thus:

	Inns.	Not Out	Runs	100s	50s	Highest Inns.	Aver.
1905	54	3	1317	2	4	155	25.82
1906	53	6	1913	4	10	162*	40.70
1907	63	6	2135	4	15	166*	37.45
1907–08 (in Australia)	22	1	876	2	6	115	41.71
1908	53	2	1904	6	7	161	37.33
1909	54	2	2114	6	7	205	40.65
1909–10 (in South Africa)	20	1	1194	3	7	187	62.84
1910	63	3	1982	3	14	133	33.03
1911	60	3	2376	4	13	154*	41.68
1911–12 (in Australia)	18	1	943	3	2	187	55.47
1912	60	6	2042	3	14	111	37.81
1913	57	5	2605	9	12	184	50.09
1913–14 (in South Africa)	22	2	1489	5	8	170	74.45
1914	48	2	2697	11	6	226	58.63
1919	49	6	2594	8	14	205*	60.32
1920	50	2	2827	11	13	215	58.89
1920–21 (in Australia)	19	1	924	4	2	131	51.33
1921	6	2	312	1	1	172*	78.00
1922	46	5	2552	10	9	168	62.24
1923	59	4	2087	5	8	136	37.94
1924	43	7	2094	6	10	211	58.16
1924–25 (in Australia)	17	1	865	3	5	154	54.06
1925	48	5	3024	16	5	266*	70.32
1926	41	3	2949	10	12	316*	77.60
1927	32	1	1641	7	5	150	52.93

*Signifies not out

Statistics

	Inns.	Not Out	Runs	100s	50s	Highest Inns.	Aver.
1928	38	7	2542	12	10	200*	82.00
1928–29 (in Australia)	18	1	962	2	7	142	56.58
1929	39	5	2263	10	8	204	66.55
1930	43	2	2103	5	14	146*	51.29
1931	49	6	2418	10	7	153	56.23
1932	35	4	1764	5	9	161*	56.90
1933	18	0	1105	6	3	221	61.38
1934	18	1	624	1	4	116	36.70
Totals	1315	106	61,237	197	271	316*	50.65

AGGREGATES

	Inns.	Not Out	Runs	100s	50s	Highest Inns.	Aver.
In England	1179	98	53,984	175	234	316*	49.93
In Australia	94	5	4570	14	22	187	51.34
In South Africa	42	3	2683	8	15	187	68.79
Totals	1315	106	61,237	197	271	316*	50.65

METHODS OF DISMISSAL

Bowled	.	.	.	286
Caught	.	.	.	695
Lbw	.	.	.	125
Run out	.	.	.	31
Stumped	.	.	.	66
Hit Wicket	.	.	.	6
Total	.	.	.	1209

He scored 5410 runs and fifteen centuries in sixty-one Test Matches, thus:

	Tests	Inns.	Not Outs	Runs	100s	50s	Highest Inns.	Aver
Australia	41	71	4	3636	12	15	187	44.2
South Africa	18	29	3	1562	2	12	211	50.0
West Indies	2	2	0	212	1	1	159	106.0
Totals	61	102	7	5410	15	28	211	56.9

*Signifies not out

Statistics

	Matches	Inns.	Not Outs	Runs	100s	50s	Highest Inns.	Aver.
1907–08 (Australia)	4	8	1	302	0	3	83	43.14
1909 (Australia)	3	6	1	132	0	1	62*	26.40
1909–10 (South Africa)	5	9	1	539	1	4	187	67.37
1911–12 (Australia)	5	9	1	662	3	1	187	82.75
1912 (Australia)	3	4	0	224	1	1	107	56.00
1912 (South Africa)	3	5	1	163	0	2	68	40.75
1913–14 (South Africa)	5	8	1	443	0	4	97	63.28
1920–21 (Australia)	5	10	0	505	2	1	123	50.50
1921 (Australia) ret'd ill	1	—	—	—	—	—	—	—
1924 (South Africa)	4	5	0	355	1	1	211	71.00
1924–25 (Australia)	5	9	0	573	3	2	154	63.66
1926 (Australia)	5	7	1	486	2	2	1·19	81.00
1928 (West Indies)	2	2	0	212	1	1	159	106.00
1928–29 (Australia)	5	9	0	451	1	2	142	50.11
1929 (South Africa)	1	2	0	62	0	1	52	31.00
1930 (Australia)	5	9	0	301	0	2	78	33.44
Totals	61	102	7	5410	15	28	211	56.94

BY INNINGS

v Australia (41 matches)

1907–08	Second Test (Melbourne) .	.	.	83 and 28
in	Third Test (Adelaide) .	.	.	26 and 23*
Australia	Fourth Test (Melbourne) .	.	.	57 and 0
	Fifth Test (Sydney) .	.	. .	72 and 13
1909	First Test (Birmingham) .	.	.	0 and 62*
in	Second Test (Lord's) .	.	.	19 and 9
England	Third Test (Leeds) .	.	.	12 and 30
1911–12	First Test (Sydney) .	.	.	63 and 22
in	Second Test (Melbourne) .	.	.	6 and 126*
Australia	Third Test (Adelaide) .	.	.	187 and 3
	Fourth Test (Melbourne) .	.	.	178
	Fifth Test (Sydney) .	.	.	32 and 45
1912	First Test (Lord's) .	.	.	107
in	Second Test (Manchester) .	.	.	19
England	Third Test (The Oval) .	.	.	66 and 32

*Signifies not out

Statistics

1920–21	First Test (Sydney) .	.	.	.	49 and 59
in	Second Test (Melbourne) .	.	.	.	122 and 120
Australia	Third Test (Adelaide)	.	.	.	18 and 123
	Fourth Test (Melbourne) .	.	.	.	27 and 13
	Fifth Test (Sydney) .	.	.	.	40 and 34
1921	Third Test (Leeds) .	.	.	.	Absent ill
in					
England					
1924–25	First Test (Sydney) .	.	.	.	115 and 57
in	Second Test (Melbourne) .	.	.	.	154 and 22
Australia	Third Test (Adelaide)	.	.	.	119 and 27
	Fourth Test (Melbourne) .	.	.	.	66
	Fifth Test (Sydney) .	.	.	.	0 and 13
1926	First Test (Nottingham) .	.	.	.	19*
in	Second Test (Lord's)	.	.	.	119
England	Third Test (Leeds) .	.	.	.	49 and 88
	Fourth Test (Manchester) .	.	.	.	74
	Fifth Test (The Oval)	.	.	.	37 and 100
1928–29	First Test (Brisbane) .	.	.	.	49 and 11
in	Second Test (Sydney)	.	.	.	40
Australia	Third Test (Melbourne)	.	.	.	20 and 49
	Fourth Test (Adelaide)	.	.	.	74 and 1
	Fifth Test (Melbourne)	.	.	.	142 and 65
1930	First Test (Nottingham) .	.	.	.	78 and 74
in	Second Test (Lord's) .	.	.	.	1 and 19
England	Third Test (Leeds) .	.	.	.	29 and 13
	Fourth Test (Manchester) .	.	.	.	31
	Fifth Test (The Oval)	.	.	.	47 and 9

v South Africa (18 matches)

1909–10	First Test (Johannesburg) .	.	.	89 and 35
in	Second Test (Durban)	.	.	53 and 70
South Africa	Third Test (Johannesburg)	.	.	11 and 93*
	Fourth Test (Cape Town) .	.	.	1 and 0
	Fifth Test (Cape Town)	.	.	187
1912	First Test (Lord's) .	.	.	.	4
in	Second Test (Leeds) .	.	.	.	27 and 55
England	Third Test (The Oval) .	.	.	.	68 and 9*

*Signifies not out

126

1913–14 in South Africa	First Test (Durban) .			82	
	Second Test (Johannesburg)	.	.	23	
	Third Test (Johannesburg)	.	.	92 and	41
	Fourth Test (Durban) .	.	.	64 and	97
	Fifth Test (Port Elizabeth)	.	.	33 and	11*
1924 in England	First Test (Birmingham) .	.	.	76	
	Second Test (Lord's)	.	.	211	
	Third Test (Leeds)	.	.	31 and	7
	Fifth Test (The Oval)	.	.	30	
1929 in England	Fifth Test (The Oval)	.	.	10 and	52

v West Indies (2 matches)

1928 in England	Second Test (Manchester) .	.	.	53
	Third Test (The Oval) .	.	.	159

He scored 197 centuries in first-class cricket: the fiftieth, 170 *v* Cape Province, 21.11.1913; the hundredth, 116 *v* Somerset, 8.5.1923; the hundred-and-fiftieth, 114 *v* Nottinghamshire on 28.5.1928, and the last (197th) *v* Lancashire 28.5.1934. From the start of his career, in 1905, to the end, in 1934, he scored at least one century in every English season and on every tour. He scored hundreds against every English county, both Universities; M.C.C.; the three countries of his Test experience—Australia, South Africa and West Indies—for Players *v* Gentlemen and Rest *v* Champion County. Of his 197 hundreds, 175 were made in England; 132 after the First World War and following his thirty-sixth birthday; 98 of them after the age of forty. Six times he scored a hundred in each innings of a match; twice, in 1920 and 1925, hundreds in each of four consecutive innings. His 316 not out for Surrey against Middlesex, 28 and 30.8.1926 is the highest individual innings in a match at Lord's; his 266 not out at Scarborough 3 and 4.9.1925, the

*Signifies not out

highest ever scored for either side in a Gentlemen *v* Players match.

The details of his first-class hundreds are:

1905 (2)
155   Surrey *v* Essex, at The Oval
102   Surrey *v* Essex, at Leyton

1906 (4)
162*   Surrey *v* Worcestershire, at The Oval
130   Surrey *v* Essex, at Leyton
125   Surrey *v* Worcestershire, at Worcester
103   Surrey *v* Middlesex, at The Oval

1907 (4)
166*   Surrey *v* Worcestershire, at The Oval
150*   Surrey *v* Warwickshire, at The Oval
135   Surrey *v* Hampshire, at Southampton
110   Surrey *v* Worcestershire, at Worcester

1907-08 (2)
115   M.C.C. Team *v* Victoria, at Melbourne
104   M.C.C. Team *v* Tasmania, at Launceston

1908 (6)
161   Surrey *v* Hampshire, at The Oval
155   Surrey *v* Kent, at The Oval
125   Surrey *v* Northamptonshire, at Northampton
117*   Surrey *v* Notts, at Nottingham
106   Surrey *v* Kent, at Blackheath
102   Surrey *v* Oxford University, at The Oval

1909 (6)
205   Surrey *v* Hampshire, at The Oval
162   Surrey *v* Hampshire, at Bournemouth
160}
100}   Surrey *v* Warwickshire, at Birmingham
159   Surrey *v* Warwickshire, at The Oval
133   Surrey *v* Gloucestershire, at Bristol

1909-10 (3)
187   England *v* South Africa, at Cape Town
163   M.C.C. Team *v* Natal, at Durban
114   M.C.C. Team *v* Western Province, at Cape Town

*Signifies not out

Statistics

1910 (3)
133   Surrey *v* Derbyshire, at Derby
119   Surrey *v* Oxford University, at The Oval
116   Surrey *v* Leicestershire, at Leicester

1911 (4)
154* Players *v* Gentlemen, at Lord's
127   Surrey *v* Leicestershire, at Leicester
117* M.C.C.'s Australian XI *v* Lord Londesborough's XI,
      at Scarborough
117   Surrey *v* Lancashire, at The Oval

1911–12 (3)
187   England *v* Australia, at Adelaide
178   England *v* Australia, at Melbourne
126* England *v* Australia, at Melbourne

1912 (3)
111   Surrey *v* Lancashire, at Manchester
107   England *v* Australia, at Lord's
104   Surrey *v* Notts, at Nottingham

1913 (9)
184   Surrey *v* Worcestershire, at Worcester
150* Surrey *v* Scotland, at The Oval
144* Surrey *v* Middlesex, at The Oval
136* Surrey *v* Northamptonshire, at Northampton
122   Surrey *v* Warwickshire, at Birmingham
115   Surrey *v* Kent, at The Oval
109   Surrey *v* Hampshire, at Southampton
107   Surrey *v* Gloucestershire, at Bristol

1913–14 (5)
170   M.C.C. Team *v* Cape Province, at Port Elizabeth
141   M.C.C. Team *v* Griqualand West, at Kimberley
137   M.C.C. Team *v* Eleven of Transvaal, at
      Vogelfontein
131* M.C.C. Team *v* Transvaal, at Johannesburg
102   M.C.C. Team *v* Transvaal, at Johannesburg

1914 (11)
226   Surrey *v* Notts, at The Oval
215* Surrey *v* Essex, at Leyton

*Signifies not out

202 Surrey *v* Yorkshire, at Lord's
183 Surrey *v* Warwickshire, at The Oval
163 Surrey *v* Hampshire, at The Oval
156 Players *v* Gentlemen, at The Oval
142 Surrey *v* Lancashire, at The Oval
141 Surrey *v* Gloucestershire, at The Oval
126 Surrey *v* Worcestershire, at Worcester
122 Surrey *v* Kent, at Blackheath
100 Surrey *v* Yorkshire, at Bradford

1919 (8)
205* Surrey *v* Australian Imperial Forces, at The Oval
120* Players *v* Gentlemen, at The Oval
116 Players *v* Gentlemen, at Scarborough
113 Players *v* Gentlemen, at Lord's
106 Surrey *v* Lancashire, at The Oval
102 Surrey *v* Kent, at Blackheath
102 Surrey *v* Lancashire, at Manchester
101 Rest of England *v* Yorkshire, at The Oval

1920 (11)
215 Rest of England *v* Middlesex, at The Oval
169 Surrey *v* Hampshire, at Southampton
138 Players *v* Gentlemen, at Scarborough
134 Surrey *v* Leicestershire, at Leicester
132 Surrey *v* Kent, at The Oval
122 Surrey *v* Warwickshire, at The Oval
115 Players of the South *v* Gentlemen of the South, at The Oval
114 Surrey *v* Northamptonshire, at Northampton
112 Surrey *v* Yorkshire, at Sheffield
110 Surrey *v* Sussex, at The Oval
101 Surrey *v* Warwickshire, at Birmingham

1920–21 (4)
131 M.C.C. Team *v* Victoria, at Melbourne
123 England *v* Australia, at Adelaide
122 England *v* Australia, at Melbourne
112 M.C.C. Team *v* New South Wales, at Sydney

1921 (1)
172* Surrey *v* Yorkshire, at Leeds

1922 (10)
168 Surrey *v* Warwickshire, at Birmingham

*Signifies not out

151* Surrey *v* Notts, at Nottingham
145 Surrey *v* Leicestershire, at Leicester
143 Surrey *v* Gloucestershire, at The Oval
140 Players *v* Gentlemen, at Lord's
139 Surrey *v* Gloucestershire, at Bristol
126 Surrey *v* Middlesex, at Lord's
112 Surrey *v* Middlesex, at The Oval
102 Surrey *v* Essex, at The Oval
100 Rest of England *v* Yorkshire, at The Oval

1923 (5)
136 Surrey *v* Middlesex, at The Oval
116* Surrey *v* Somerset, at Bath
105 Surrey *v* Notts, at The Oval
105 Players *v* Gentlemen, at Scarborough
104 Surrey *v* Lancashire, at The Oval

1924 (6)
211 England *v* South Africa, at Lord's
203* Surrey *v* Notts, at Nottingham
118* Surrey *v* Derbyshire, at The Oval
118 Players *v* Gentlemen, at Lord's
105 Surrey *v* Gloucestershire, at The Oval
105 Surrey *v* Notts, at The Oval

1924–25 (3)
154 England *v* Australia, at Melbourne
119 England *v* Australia, at Adelaide
115 England *v* Australia, at Sydney

1925 (16)
266* Players *v* Gentlemen, at Scarborough
215 Surrey *v* Warwickshire, at Birmingham
189 Surrey *v* Notts, at Nottingham
143*⎫
104 ⎭ Surrey *v* Cambridge University, at The Oval
140 Players *v* Gentlemen, at Lord's
129 Surrey *v* Essex, at Leyton
120 Surrey *v* Warwickshire, at The Oval
111 Surrey *v* Somerset, at The Oval
109 Surrey *v* Glamorgan, at The Oval
107 Surrey *v* Essex, at The Oval
106 Rest of England *v* Yorkshire, at The Oval
105 Surrey *v* Kent, at Blackheath

*Signifies not out

131

104 Surrey *v* Gloucestershire, at The Oval
101*⎫
101 ⎭ Surrey *v* Somerset, at Taunton

1926 (10)
316* Surrey *v* Middlesex, at Lord's
261 Surrey *v* Oxford University, at The Oval
200 Surrey *v* Hampshire, at Southampton
176* Surrey *v* Middlesex, at The Oval
163 Players *v* Gentlemen, at Lord's
119 England *v* Australia, at Lord's
112 Surrey *v* Gloucestershire, at The Oval
108 Surrey *v* Cambridge University, at The Oval
102 Surrey *v* Yorkshire, at The Oval
100 England *v* Australia, at The Oval

1927 (7)
150 Surrey *v* Yorkshire, at The Oval
146 Surrey *v* New Zealanders, at The Oval
131 Surrey *v* Notts, at The Oval
121 Surrey *v* Kent, at Blackheath
119 Players *v* Gentlemen, at Scarborough
112⎫
104⎭ Surrey *v* Hampshire, at The Oval

1928 (12)
200* Surrey *v* Warwickshire, at Birmingham
159 England *v* West Indies, at The Oval
150 Rest of England *v* Lancashire, at The Oval
124 Surrey *v* Gloucestershire, at The Oval
123* Surrey *v* West Indies, at The Oval
119* Mr H. D. G. Leveson Gower's XI *v* West Indies, at Scarborough
117 Surrey *v* Northamptonshire, at Northampton
114 Surrey *v* Notts, at Nottingham
109 Surrey *v* Kent, at The Oval
105 Surrey *v* Yorkshire, at The Oval
101 Surrey *v* Leicestershire, at The Oval
100* Surrey *v* M.C.C., at Lord's

1928–29 (2)
142 England *v* Australia, at Melbourne
101 M.C.C. *v* South Australia, at Adelaide

*Signifies not out

Statistics

1929 (10)
204 Surrey *v* Somerset, at The Oval
154 Surrey *v* Hampshire, at The Oval
151 Mr C. I. Thornton's XI *v* South Africans, at Scarborough
150* Surrey *v* Kent, at Blackheath
134 Surrey *v* Somerset, at Weston-super-Mare
128 Surrey *v* Glamorgan, at Cardiff
118 Surrey *v* Kent, at The Oval
115* Surrey *v* Leicestershire, at The Oval
111 Surrey *v* Middlesex, at Lord's
102* Surrey *v* Essex, at The Oval

1930 (5)
146* Surrey *v* Australians, at The Oval
137 ⎫
111*⎬ Surrey *v* Glamorgan, at The Oval
106 Surrey *v* Sussex, at Hastings
100 Surrey *v* Leicestershire, at The Oval

1931 (10)
153 Mr H. D. G. Leveson Gower's XI *v* New Zealanders,
    at Scarborough
147 Surrey *v* Warwickshire, at The Oval
144 Players *v* Gentlemen, at Scarborough
133* Surrey *v* Yorkshire, at The Oval
128 Surrey *v* Somerset, at The Oval
117 Surrey *v* Sussex, at The Oval
110 Players *v* Gentlemen, at The Oval
106 Surrey *v* Glamorgan, at The Oval
105 Surrey *v* Derbyshire, at Chesterfield
101* Surrey *v* Somerset, at Taunton

1932 (5)
161* Players *v* Gentlemen, at Lord's
123 Surrey *v* Somerset, at Taunton
113 ⎫
119*⎬ Surrey *v* Essex, at The Oval
111 Surrey *v* Middlesex, at Lord's

1933 (6)
221 Surrey *v* West Indies, at The Oval
133 Surrey *v* Nottinghamshire, at The Oval
118 Surrey *v* Cambridge University, at The Oval
117 Surrey *v* Somerset, at The Oval

*Signifies not out

133

101 Surrey *v* Kent, at Blackheath
100 Surrey *v* Warwickshire, at The Oval

1934 (1)
116 Surrey *v* Lancashire, at Manchester

He also scored forty-seven hundreds in minor Cricket; including two for Cambridgeshire, two in one Surrey trial match, four for M.C.C. against junior teams overseas; four for R.A.F.; four for the Maharajah of Vizianagram's XI.

CENTURY OPENING PARTNERSHIPS

Hobbs shared in a century opening stand, on average, once in every eight innings he played; 163 altogether, with fourteen different partners. There were forty with Tom Hayward (in 1907 the two shared four three-figure opening partnerships in a week); sixty-three with Andrew Sandham; twenty-six with Herbert Sutcliffe, thirteen with Wilfred Rhodes; six with Donald Knight; three with Jack Russell; two each with George Gunn and Percy Holmes; one each with Charles Fry, Albert Baker, Ernie Hayes, Miles Howell, Andrew Ducat and Bob Gregory. Of his twenty-three opening partnerships of over 100 in Tests, fifteen were with Herbert Sutcliffe, eight with Wilfred Rhodes (their 323 at Melbourne in 1911–12, for long the highest in all Test cricket, remains the highest in Anglo-Australian Tests). Those of over 250 were:

428	A. Sandham, Surrey *v* Oxford University, Oval	..	1926
352	T. Hayward, Surrey *v* Warwickshire, Oval ..	..	1909
323	W. Rhodes, England *v* Australia, Melbourne ..	..	1911–12
313	T. Hayward, Surrey *v* Worcestershire, Worcester	..	1913
290	T. Hayward, Surrey *v* Yorkshire, Lord's ..	..	1914
283	H. Sutcliffe, England *v* Australia, Melbourne ..	..	1924–25
268	H. Sutcliffe, England *v* South Africa, Lord's ..	..	1924
264	A. Sandham, Surrey *v* Somerset, Taunton	..	1932
253	A. Sandham, Surrey *v* West Indies, Oval..	..	1928

Hobbs bowled medium pace, generally outswing; and, in three Test Matches in South Africa in 1909–10, he opened both the batting and the bowling for England. In all first-class cricket he took 113 wickets (at 23.97) and made 317 catches.

Bibliography

Altham, H. S. & Swanton, E. W.: *A History of Cricket* (Allen & Unwin 1938)

Crawford, J. N.: *Trip to 'Kangaroo' Land* (Cricket Offices 1909)

Fender, P. G. H.: *Defending The Ashes* (Chapman & Hall 1921)
The Turn of the Wheel (Faber 1929)
The Tests of 1930 (Faber 1930)

Hobbs, J. B.: *Recovering The Ashes* (Pitman 1912)
My Cricket Memories (Heinemann 1924)
Playing for England (Gollancz 1931)
My Life Story (*The Star* 1935)

Leveson Gower, Sir H. D. G.: *Cricket Personalities* (Williams & Norgate 1925)
Off and On the Field (Stanley Paul 1953)

Maclaren, A. C.: *The Perfect Batsman: J. B. Hobbs in Action* (Cassell 1926)

Mailey, A. A.: *10 for 66 and All That* (Phoenix House 1958)

Trevor, P.: *With the M.C.C. in Australia (1907–1908)* (Alston Rivers 1908)

Warner, Sir Pelham: *England v Australia* (Mills & Boon 1912)
Cricket Reminiscences (G. Richards 1920)
Cricket Between Two Wars (Chatto & Windus 1942)
Long Innings (Harrap 1951)

Wisden Cricketers' Almanack v.y.

Index

Compiled by J. D. Coldham

139

Index

Index

Index

Index